X

Paul Scott's *Raj Quartet*:
History and Division

PETER CHILDS

Paul Scott's *Raj Quartet*:
History and Division

English Literary Studies
University of Victoria
1998

ENGLISH LITERARY STUDIES
Published at the University of Victoria

Founding Editor
Samuel L. Macey

ISBN 0-920604-61-7

The ELS Monograph Series is published in consultation with members of the Department by ENGLISH LITERARY STUDIES, Department of English, University of Victoria, P.O. Box 3070, Victoria, B.C., Canada, v8w 3w1.

ELS Monograph Series No. 77
© 1998 by Peter Childs

CONTENTS

ACKNOWLEDGMENTS

I should like to thank the British Academy for funding a study visit to the United States, thereby enabling me to consult Scott's unpublished work. With respect to that visit, I must also express my gratitude to Cathy Henderson and the staff at the Harry Ransom Humanities Research Center at Austin and to Sidney F. Huttner and his staff at Tulsa's McFarlin Library, for both their warm welcome and their unfailing assistance. I wish also to thank Mrs. Avery-Scott and David Higham Associates for permission to quote from Scott's novels and to reproduce material from the Scott archives.

Additional thanks go to Robert M. Schuler and the readers who very helpfully commented on the book in manuscript form at English Literary Studies. I should also like to acknowledge the helpful comments and advice of Patrick Swinden and Roger Pooley, as well as the invaluable support of Andor Gomme, who first introduced me to *The Raj Quartet* many years ago, and who has provided both criticism and enthusiasm for my work on Scott ever since. This book is dedicated to him.

A version of the conclusion appeared in *The Journal of Indian Writing in English*, 24:1, January 1996. All previously unpublished material by Paul Scott in this book is © N. E. Avery-Scott, 1998, reproduced by permission of David Higham Associates Limited.

NOTE ON REFERENCES
AND UNPUBLISHED MATERIAL

Where Scott has offered a particular spelling of an Indian word (e.g. *suttee*, not *sati*) this has been adopted throughout the book. Otherwise, spellings, though consistent for the use of any particular word, are suited to their contexts. Citations from *The Raj Quartet*, Scott's other published works, and Bakhtin's writings are all included in the body of the text. Abbreviations of Scott's works referred to in the text are as follows:

A—*The Alien Sky*
B—*The Birds of Paradise*
C—*The Corrida at San Felíu*
D—*A Division of the Spoils*
J—*The Jewel in the Crown*
L—*The Chinese Love Pavilion*
M—*My Appointment with the Muse*
S—*The Day of the Scorpion*
T—*The Towers of Silence*

Abbreviations of Bakhtin's works used in the text are as follows:

DI—*The Dialogic Imagination*, ed. Michael Holquist. Trans. Caryl Emerson and Michael Holquist. Austin: University of Texas Press, 1981.

SG—*Speech Genres and Other Late Essays*, ed. Caryl Emerson and Michael Holquist. Trans. Vern W. McGee. Austin: University of Texas Press, 1986.

AA—*Art and Answerability*, ed. Michael Holquist and Vadim Liapunov. Trans. Vadim Liapunov. Supplement translated by Kenneth Brostrom. Austin: University of Texas Press, 1990.

PDP—*Problems of Dostoevsky's Poetics*, ed. and trans. by Caryl Emerson. Manchester: Manchester University Press, 1984.

RW—*Rabelais and his World*. Trans. Hélène Iswolsky. Bloomington: Indiana University Press, 1984.

The book includes discussion of unpublished material taken from Scott's manuscripts, correspondence, and drafts for essays and reviews. These documents are housed at two locations: at the Harry Ransom Research Center of the University of Texas, Austin (referred to as Austin throughout the book), and at the Special Collections department of the McFarlin Library at the University of Tulsa (referred to as Tulsa).

Of importance to the research for this book, there are at Austin eleven manuscript versions of *The Jewel in the Crown*, five of *The Day of the Scorpion*, six of *The Towers of Silence*, and seven of *A Division of the Spoils*. References to this material will cite the number of the manuscript, as given by Austin, and a page reference where one is present (e.g. page 23 of version six of *The Towers of Silence* will be given as *The Towers of Silence*: Austin: 6: 23).

At Tulsa, there is a sizable collection of material in large document boxes: twenty boxes of correspondence (kept as Series I); nine of manuscripts of *Staying On*, lectures, essays, and plays (Series II); and eight of book reviews and readers' reports (Series III). Tulsa uses a straightforward reference system of Series: Box: File (e.g. Tulsa: III: 2: 4) to refer to the location of a particular item, and this has been employed wherever necessary. If a page number is applicable, this has also been added (e.g. Scott, "India: A Post-Forsterian View" [Tulsa: II: 7: 10: 26]). Where I have been aware of a published reference to material I have used, it has been cited, and this applies also to references where I have made use of a fuller or overlapping quotation.

INTRODUCTION

Critical views on Paul Scott's *The Raj Quartet* have varied enormously.[1] Edward Said uses the epithet "great" and M. M. Mahood describes it as "an imaginative creation of Tolstoyan breadth and depth," while William Walsh decides it is "not an authentic literary experience of a particularly significant kind."[2] The British historian Antony Copley argues that the *Quartet* is "quite possibly the best novel we are likely to get on that whole mixed sad tale of decolonization," while the Sri Lankan writer, Tarzie Vittachi, believes that Scott did for India what "Dostoevsky did for the Russia of his time, and Gabriel García Márquez for the Andes of his."[3] The only consensus to be found reflects Margaret Scanlan's sentiment that the *Quartet* is "impeccably researched historical fiction" (135).

In the discussions that follow, the historical dimensions to the *Quartet* will be kept firmly in focus. The first four chapters of this study examine those historical frameworks within which Scott encourages the reader to approach the text. Chapter one considers the *Quartet*'s relation to earlier English anti-colonial fiction in order to provide one dimension to a literary-historical background and to explore the common issues of these texts together with some of the current critical debates that surround them. The second chapter begins from several co-ordinates of religious history, and its subject is the *Quartet*'s mythopoeic dimension. Stories of paradise and the Fall are used by Scott to approach the nadir of the crisis of faith which had been undermining the raj since the middle of the nineteenth century and which paralleled a decline in belief in Britain's authority, mission, and purpose in India. The next chapter considers the philosophy of history which is most relevant to the tetralogy, Emerson's, and the way Scott integrates it into the final shape and form of the *Quartet*. Chapter four outlines the aspects of political history that Scott uses to come nearer to what Merrick would call the "situation" of the British-Indian relationship under the raj. Without directly describing events such as the "Mutiny" of 1857, Scott incorporates his view of their significance into his reconstruction of the years 1942-47.

Subsequent chapters use, to varying degrees, the theories of the Russian critic Mikhail Bakhtin to examine particular characters in the *Quartet* together with the issues that the narration builds around them. Three chapters expand on the areas of doubt, uncertainty, parallax, and prejudicial commentary that earlier chapters identified, while viewing themes such as division and racism in terms of Bakhtin's critical theories of dialogism and perception of the Other. The concluding chapter introduces Bakhtin's theory of carnival to assess Scott's introduction of humour into his portrait of post-colonial India. It views *Staying On* as a text in dialogue with the *Quartet.*

Bakhtin's theories hinge on considerations of the historical context into which utterances are inserted, and this raises the question why Scott wrote about the raj over twenty years after its dissolution. One important answer is that the novels are socially and ideologically directed towards their own era of the sixties and seventies. As this will be alluded to in later discussions, it is worth pointing out some contemporary details of a politician with whose views the *Quartet* enters into dialogue and against whom Scott wrote on several occasions: Enoch Powell.[4] In these decades Powell was both outspoken and influential. In 1965, when Scott was working on the first volume of the *Quartet,* Powell, though with little chance of winning, stood for the Conservative Party leadership. In the year of *The Day of the Scorpion*'s publication, 1968, Powell made his infamous "rivers of blood" speech, which was followed by a gallup poll the next month that suggested 74 per cent of Britons supported his views on immigration.[5] In 1969, Powell came second to Harold Wilson in a BBC "World at One" poll of votes for "Man of the Decade."[6] Two years later, Powell's repeated calls for a massive repatriation scheme ended in the Immigration Bill which denied the right of Commonwealth workers to settle in Britain. It was not until 1972, when Scott was working on the fourth volume of the *Quartet,* that Britain's Race Relations Act came into force and Powell's personal influence, though not his ideological stance which had taken root in such organizations as the National Front (founded 1967), started slowly to decline. On publication, Scott's novels actively worked against Powell's kind of parochialism and challenged both its polemical authority and its view of history. Powell saw England's connection with India as the spur to all its other imperial efforts. Take away India, and the Empire, the idea of which Powell saw as the greatest impediment to England's self-regeneration, goes with it. "The British Empire, as we know it in political mythology," he says "was an invention" (248). Powell goes so far as to claim that, to its great cost, Britain had since 1800 been two nations, by which he means the British Isles on the one hand and British India on the other (244). Powell blames the worst moments and events of British history since that time on an over-valuation of the connection with India, and on India's role in fantasies of English identity.

As prologue to the discussions of Scott's perspective on history, I will review two areas of importance to his work in this introduction. One is his interest in the meaning, values, and death of liberal humanism, which is the political ground from which he criticizes the raj. The other is Scott's fascination with "images" in fiction.

* * *

One way to understand Scott's liberal humanism, and its connection with fiction, is in terms of a dilemma.[7] The "liberal dilemma" is explained by C. B. Cox in his introductory chapter of that title in *The Free Spirit*. He sees it as the liberal's Achilles' heel always to reject dogma, allegiance to tradition (religious or secular), and extreme political action or commitment—because they too often end in tyranny and violence. He says the "aim of the liberal humanist is not service of party or creed, but self-fulfilment [and yet] the liberal emphasis on motives and consequences has often led to sterility" (7). Cox argues, for example, that in E. M. Forster's art, as in his life, it leads to exclusion and withdrawal, as in *A Passage to India*.

A comparison between Scott and Forster, which is suggested by the common subject of the raj in their finest novels, is made inevitable by their shared interest in liberal humanism and the liberal dilemma. Scott wrote the following in a 1966 review of a new edition of *A Passage to India*:

> [In the novel Forster writes about] the failure that was inherent, always, in Fieldingism. It was a failure which only Fieldingism itself, in its most intelligent form, could intelligently become aware of. It is this self-awareness of failure as inevitable but darkly mysterious that makes *A Passage to India* not only one of the great tragic works of twentieth-century fiction but one that we have still not wholly grown into, let alone grown out of. The failure of Fieldingism or, to give it its other name, the failure of liberal humanism, is a modern, in fact rather pressing problem, actively in search of solution. The reasons for the failure are not yet understood, but the failure itself impinges on us at every turn we try to take.[8]

Scott continued to grapple with this problem, and by the time he came to draft an article on Forster and India, he saw it in terms of the liberal dilemma:

> between them, Mrs. Moore, Fielding and—up to a catalytic point, Miss Quested—act out for us what has been called the liberal dilemma—the dilemma of liberal-minded people when challenged to stand up and be counted and prove that, in the world of affairs, the liberal idea would work.

The dilemma lies in the fact that the liberal idea could never enlist naked power in its service. Not to see the other person's point of view is bad enough; to crush it by force is impossible. One relies, in the end, on the solid bourgeois vote. It was such a vote in the House of Commons—almost, as it were, between Question Time and Other Business—that achieved the English liberal purpose in India.[9]

Scott was often less concerned with arguing the wrongs of the British Empire as an institution than with discussing the manner of its dissolution. He believed the raj to have been morally untenable, even according to the morals of most imperialists, since the First World War; but there remained the responsibility for the agenda and priorities of its dismantling. The dereliction of responsibility in the devolution of power is therefore the chief political concern of the *Quartet*.

In social terms, Terry Eagleton argues that liberal humanism is the "conscience of bourgeois society, gentle, sensitive, and ineffectual . . . concerned with the uniqueness of the individual, the imperishable truths of the human condition [and] the sensuous textures of lived experience."[10] This also seems to delineate the liberal dilemma. Scott's concern with the end of liberal humanism is very much with "conscience" and with what he thought was replacing the liberal conscience in Western society after the Second World War: prejudice and dogmatism.

With regard to the Empire and the raj, Scott was acutely aware of the history of two creeds at work within the administration of India: liberalism and paternalism. He described the development of the latter in this way: "the general flow of history as it emerged from the age of Humanism and self-seeking into the age of Evangelicalism and Utilitarianism, the twin forces that combined to produce paternalism both at home and abroad (progress on the one hand, the White Man's Burden on the other)."[11] Conscious of the collapse of liberalism in Britain in the sixties, he felt that paternalism was at the root of contemporary views on immigration and racial discrimination, and consequently he wanted to understand the end of liberal humanism as a counterforce. His chief concerns were therefore with comprehending liberalism's loss of agency and the legacy of that breakdown. Scott partly details the closing years of the raj in an attempt to understand how both the triumph and downfall of liberal humanist policy were situated in the eventual release of India. Both, because while the sub-continent was given freedom by the means of a vote, Independence was accompanied by insufficient concern or desire for a united India. As a result, Scott's view of the post-colonial world reflects his construction of the failure of the raj: "Euro-

14

peanism was ending in the Berlin Wall; anti-colonialism in partition; the ideal of world-citizenship in proliferating nationalism; liberal humanism in what we know today as black tyranny and white backlash."[12]

For Scott, the inadequacies of liberal humanism gave perspectives on past failures and future dangers. Firstly, he saw British colonialism as having been a struggle between the viewpoints of paternalists and liberal humanists. He believed humanism had triumphed in the Parliamentary vote to end the raj; but humanism had also shown its failure there too because Britain left India divided and at war with itself. Secondly, Scott was anxious over what was emerging to replace liberal humanism in the sixties and seventies, when Powellism was gaining support in Britain and war was breaking out between the raj's inheritors: India and Pakistan were at war in 1965, and then again in 1971.[13] It seemed that the failed liberal humanist beliefs in unity and uncertainty were simply being replaced by worsening religious intolerance and the certainties of racism.

This is a brief outline of the attitude behind Scott's portrayal of the end of the raj and why it was important to him both historically and in terms of its aftermath. It will be necessary to return to this throughout the following chapters, but to balance this introduction I will now turn from history to fiction, and to the fundamental novelistic device of the *Quartet*: the "image."

It is often maintained that there are two fundamental categories of imagery in literature: the literal and the figurative. Literal imagery most commonly produces an effect through repetition or intensity (the fog and the rain in the opening chapters of *Bleak House* are the actual weather conditions, but they are also images of confusion and misery, accentuated by their severity). Figurative imagery achieves its ends by the striking quality of being significantly different from but also curiously or revealingly similar to its object (the extreme case is the conceit).

Scott refers to something noticeably different by his use of the term "image." For him, it does not mean an image of something—neither literal nor figurative—but a memorable picture which, as one in a sequence, evokes feelings and meanings associated with the events that surround these isolated stills:

> Carton at the guillotine, Lord Jim standing apart from his fellow officers in the streets of Singapore, Constance Chatterley making her bosky way to the gamekeeper's cottage, the cry going up for Esmiss Esmoor from the crowd outside the courtroom in *A Passage to India*—these are what these novels are to a reader. They may be different things to different readers, but they will

15

always be particularized and often solitary images of a human reality, exemplifying the book.   (M 82)

For Scott, any major part of a novel always evolved from one starting-point: an image which would carry the symbolic weight of the larger story and which would accumulate associations as the narrative built other images upon it. Scott wrote about this technique on several occasions:

> The major problem the novelist has is so to construct his books as to provoke, in what I [call] that area of meeting or confrontation of his own and the reader's mind, a series of images from which the reader will extract a notion of human reality.   (M 82)

> A novel is a sequence of images. In sequence these images tell a story. . . . Constructing a novel—telling a tale, for me at any rate—is not a business of thinking of a story, arranging it in a certain order and then finding images to fit it. The images come first. I may have a general notion of wanting to write a book about a certain time, or place, but unless the general notion is given the impetus of an image that seems to be connected, the notion never gets off the ground.   (M 54)

Scott speaks of a sequence of images, but this is far from being the sequence of events, the "series of gig-lamps symmetrically arranged" that Virginia Woolf decried in the novels of Bennett and Galsworthy ("Modern Fiction" 88). It is more akin to a picture encompassed by meaning like Conrad's misty halo "enveloping the tale" (*Heart of Darkness* 8): what meaning there is, lies not in the image of an event but in what surrounds it by association. The distinction is extremely important and is necessary in order not to misunderstand Scott's methodology. For example, in *The Edwardian Novelists* John Batchelor maintains that Scott is one of the "Bond-street tailors" such as Bennett, whom Woolf attacks in her essay on "Modern Fiction":

> Bennett takes several dates in the lives of his characters and shows their lives at those moments, allowing the dramatic present to record the past and imply the future. But the connections between these islands of dramatized presentation are made in the omniscient, chronicle-writing manner common to Fielding, Trollope, or Cowper-Powys: the tradition that still behaves, in Powys and other twentieth- century figures such as Henry Williamson and Paul Scott, as though Modernism had never happened.   (174)

A statement such as this confuses the vast canvas painted by Bennett's texts, and also by Scott's, with the linear, chronological, didactic narration that novelists such as Bennett used, and Scott did not. The scope of

Scott's quartet of novels rivals that of any nineteenth-century triple-decker, but the techniques he uses to organize the text bear little relation. Both David Rubin (120-21) and Martin Green (336) are far nearer the mark in referring to Scott's use of a "post-Proustian form."

The misrepresentation of Scott, whose greatest influences are pro-minent modernists—James, Eliot, Conrad, and Nabokov—leads to a misrepresentation of his fiction as it wrongly suggests that he is also concerned with a nineteenth-century objectivity, restricted by New-tonian conceptions of space-time. Instead, Scott offers the reader no certainties or answers, but a number of positions relative to an incident; and he does this in order to explore how situations are constructed through different points of observation. Along these lines, Scott wrote once that his novels were "much more a series of questions than a set of statements" (M 114). His characters also reflect both a modernist sense of alienation (due to exile) and a nascent postmodernist experience of schizophrenia (due to the pervasive theme of division).

The seed of Scott's stories is always an originating image that the others grow from and not a particular argument or confident assertion. The image, if an effective one, will bear the weight of the events and meanings spiralling from it:

> *The situation, somehow, must be made to rise out of the image.*
>
> You need, to begin with, a strong central image that yields a strong situation, or series of situations. By strong I don't necessarily mean strongly dramatic. I mean strong in the sense of tenacious.   (M 54)

The image is never one of "truth," and in his reluctance to offer facts and certainties Scott resembles Forster. Events are made deliberately problematic in the *Quartet*, just as the "truth" of the Marabar caves was unknown to Forster (but for very different reasons—see chapter one). This is why the image must be simply a point of reference and cannot contain either a conclusion or an explanation. The starting point is then built upon, in a strategy Scott describes as "going in through the back of the image":

> a technique of reverse exploration, it creates scenes and situations that are variations of those of the original image. It is a technique of comparison. It is a way of giving balance to different aspects of a narrative, a way of giving form and shapeliness to the whole and extra significance to each of the parts thus compared.   (M 64)

So, while germinating in an original image, which could be a part of one idea or event but will also carry associations with many more, Scott's

17

texts accrete meaning until the novel forms an overall pattern. It does this through images, complementary to the original one, that have their own associations:

> Going in through the back of the original image has begun to unlock its mysteries, and in this particular case [*The Jewel in the Crown*]—and each novel you write is a different case—*by leading up to the climax of the riots it has suggested that the form the novel will take is that of approach*, through different eyes, through different histories, from different vantage points of time—to a central point of reference, which is exemplified in the original image—the action of that image and the implicit emotional content of that image.
>
> (M 65)

The original image in *The Jewel in the Crown* is that of a woman running. However, the image of Daphne's flight assumes a greater significance over the course of the *Quartet* because it is the generating image of the Bibighar Affair, the key incident of the four novels.

> The genesis of a novel is an image. One may even say—an apparently unrelated image. I think you'll find that most novelists who take their work seriously would agree about this. Graham Greene referred to it in connection with his novel *A Burnt-Out Case*. In the only novel I have ever written *about* a novelist, *The Corrida at San Felíu*, I illustrated this process more or less step-by-step. But the quotation I'm about to give comes from neither Greene nor my own book, but from an essay published two years ago by a young English writer called John Fowles . . . : "It started four or five months ago as a visual image. A woman stands at the end of a deserted quay and stares out to sea. That was all. This image rose in my mind one morning when I was still in bed half asleep. It corresponded to no actual incident in my life (or in art) that I can recall. . . . These mythopoeic 'stills' (they seem almost always static) float into my mind very often. I ignore them, since that is the best way of finding whether they really are the door into a new world." That is very well put and corresponds exactly with my own experience.[14]

To Scott's initial image of a woman running he adds answers to circumstantial questions: what is she running from, when is she running and where; questions which themselves generate new questions and situations. As the circumstances broaden, there are points of connection between the originating image and the surrounding events. One of Scott's most sympathetic characters, Sister Ludmila, expresses it in this way:

> There are images that stay vividly in your mind, even after many years; images coupled with the feeling that at the same time came to you. Sometimes you

can know that such an image has been selected to stay with you for ever out of the hundreds you every day encounter.   (J 122)

So the image is both a symbolic and a synecdochic but apparently unrelated representation of the emotional impact the story should have on the reader.[15] As such it is similar to Scott's overall view of fictional prose per se, only on a smaller scale. His favourite definition of the novel, which came from Walter Allen, was that it constituted "an extended metaphor of an author's view of life" (M 115). The Russian critic Mikhail Bakhtin, whose theories are used extensively later in this study, states a similar view, using his own idiosyncratic vocabulary and contextualizing the author's perspective in the historical conditions under which the text is produced:[16]

> When heteroglossia enters the novel it becomes subject to an artistic reworking. The social and historical voices populating language, all its words and all its forms, which provide language with its particular concrete conceptualizations, are organized in the novel into a structured stylistic system that expresses the differentiated socio- ideological position of the author amid the heteroglossia of the epoch.   (DI 300)

Later chapters of this discussion will elucidate Bakhtin's terminology and use the idea of heteroglossia, or competing discourses, to demonstrate how Scott engaged with many of the preoccupations of modern literature and its critics: identity, otherness, gender, nationality, the relationship between language and power, silence, and "race."[17] To end this introduction, I need now to turn to a concrete example of Scott's images and also to outline some of the variations that result from what he calls "going in through the back of the image."

The image of the woman running is the one Scott begins from—the image that generates the first sentence, the seminal event of the Bibighar Affair at Mayapore, and the four volumes of the *Quartet*, down to the lyric poem that closes *A Division of the Spoils*. That poem begins with the words "Everything means something to you." It finishes with this verse:

> Fleeting moments: these are held a long time in the eye,
> The blind eye of the ageing poet,
> So that even you, Gaffur, can imagine
> In this darkening landscape
> The bowman lovingly choosing his arrow,
> The hawk outpacing the cheetah,
> (The fountain splashing lazily in the courtyard),
> The girl running with the deer.   (D 598)

19

Everything in the poem means something to the reader, and nearly every line recalls a key image in the tetralogy. Several expressions return to the first sentence of the *Quartet*, which introduced these images:

> Imagine, then, a flat landscape, dark for the moment, but even so conveying to a girl running in the still deeper shadow cast by the wall of the Bibighar Gardens an idea of immensity, of distance, such as years before Miss Crane had been conscious of standing where a lane ended and cultivation began: a different landscape but also in the alluvial plain between the mountains of the north and the plateau of the south.   (J 1)

The repetition of the invitation to imagine, the darkening landscape, and the girl running, bring together in the mind Scott's picture of the British experience of India and the Indian experience of the raj. The young woman, Daphne, is running from the result of her attempt to cross a line that has been drawn between Indians and Anglo-Indians. It is an attempt which is repeated in the stories of Edwina Crane, Sister Ludmila, Lady Manners, Mabel Layton, Barbie Batchelor, and Sarah Layton. The arbitrary yet forceful way in which the raj separates people is the catalyst of events in the *Quartet*, from the first page through to the division of India in the final volume. Scott depicts the prejudices which cause these lines to be inscribed, whether they be ones of class, colour, "race," or religion, and graphically presents the effects—violence and flight—of attempts to cross them.[18] In this, Scott criticizes both the stated intention and the failure to unify India under the raj.

The *Quartet*'s opening sentence associates Daphne running with a feeling of immensity, both of the landscape and of the darkness. This records the estrangement in India of insular colonialists whose sense of community is marked by familiarity, belonging, and tradition, not by acceptance or tolerance. On the one hand the idea of "an alien sky" is maintained: "A phrase came into the mind. The sweet indifference of man's environment to his problems. Pathetic fallacy or no, I really felt it, an indifference to us that amounted to a contempt" (S 379). But, on the other hand, Scott broadens out the related theme of prejudice (which is a heightened form of a preference for the familiar) and shows people affected by barriers other than those between British and Indians, such as the Muslim member of the predominantly Hindu Congress, Kasim, and the socially inferior Merrick whose only chance to circumvent the barrier of class, so strong in England, is to work in the British colonies where that particular prejudice is comparatively weakened by the stronger one of race.[19]

So, the subject of the *Quartet*'s first sentence is not a woman running, but the immense landscape that connects her with another character, Miss Crane, who is also conscious of a feeling of unfamiliarity and alienation in "a landscape calculated to inspire in the most sympathetic Western heart a degree of cultural shock" (J 87). I have noted how this feeling of immensity is to be linked with British insularity and prejudice, and, accordingly, Miss Crane is pictured standing at another boundary "where a lane ended and cultivation began." This is symbolic of the boundary between the administrators of imperial capitalism and political rule, encumbered with a puzzled fascination for a vast sub-continent, and the Indian people, subject to and curious about the esoteric ways of distant, invading islanders. The boundary between them is primarily one of skin—the only physical means by which they can be joined but also the mark of their difference. Divided in this way, Britons and Indians are still locked together:

> the affair that began on the evening of August 9th, 1942, in Mayapore, ended with the spectacle of two nations in violent opposition, not for the first time nor as yet for the last because they were then still locked in an imperial embrace of such long standing and subtlety it was no longer possible for them to know whether they hated or loved one another, or what it was that held them together and seemed to have confused the image of their separate destinies. (J 1)

The *Quartet* reconstructs the final spasm of this embrace, lasting exactly five years from 9 August 1942, the day of the Bibighar, to 9 August 1947, when Guy Perron flies away from India a few days before Independence, and writes the coda of the novel. It is an embrace that characterizes Scott's own fascination for tensions that exist between dark and light skins, dark and light personalities, and for attractions in the dark and the light.[20] This is a continuation from the last passage he wrote before starting the *Quartet*, at the end of *The Corrida at San Felíu*:

> And like this we are turned suddenly to stone, because here a union, an awful wholeness has been achieved between man and nature; and so we lie forever in carved cohabitation, in the dark and in the light, in the rains, through all the seasons of the year, immortally joined and lying as still as if we were dead. . . . (C 316)

Such "awful" union—usually abortive or belated—is common in Scott's fiction and is the reason why there is a woman running at the start of the *Quartet*. In the tetralogy the embrace figures as a death-clutch but also as an attempt to grasp companionship when it is too late: Edwina Crane

21

holds the hand of the dead Mr. Chaudhuri, as Daphne holds the hand of the unconscious Hari, and, to take an example from a later volume, Mabel Layton's dead body lies in the hospital, "with its right arm raised, held by brown hands" (T 229).

The result of each of these attempts at personal union shows the forces of attraction and repulsion behind them. There is the expression of care and companionship in the embrace and there is also the reaction to the violence: Mr. Chaudhuri's murder, Hari's assault, Daphne's rape, the violent recriminations of Reid and Merrick. This reaction is allied to Scott's original image of the woman running: Daphne is running away from Hari because she insists they cannot be seen together; exploring the back of the image, it becomes Miss Crane accelerating in her car because Mr. Chaudhuri insists she must leave for her own safety, or Miss Batchelor escaping from the horrific sight of Mabel Layton's dead body as Doctor Lal shrieks that she should never have come into the hospital room. In each case, each woman in flight— Daphne Manners, Edwina Crane, Barbie Batchelor—has been set on a course that will lead to her death. So, the image of a woman running has developed into these unconnected but similar images of British women who, in the manner and urgency of their flight, are suggestive of the raj's departure and demise.

The final incident of the *Quartet* records the historical expression of this theme as one of the many train attacks of 1947 is suffered by the remaining central characters. By this time, the possibility of union has been abandoned: Britons are leaving the subcontinent, Pakistan is about to be carved from India, and Hindu-Muslim violence is rife. Appropriately, Sarah Layton has not become involved with Ahmed Kasim, as Daphne did with Hari, but, symptomatic of the time, has initiated a relationship with an Englishman, Guy Perron. Going in through the back of the images of five years earlier has left this variation: Ahmed, like Mr. Chaudhuri and Hari, is brutally attacked by Indians, and separated from his British companions. The significant alteration is that now, in 1947, the English are not the target of Indian resentment and they are treated politely, though they are still largely responsible (for the manner in which they left India, as for the imprisonment of Congress Members in 1942).[21] In Scott's eyes, Britain had chosen the time and manner of Independence yet excused itself from the consequences of devolution because India "went willingly." Ahmed voluntarily leaves the railway compartment, saving the English from possible harm, saying, "It seems to be me they want" (D 591), just as Mr. Chaudhuri voluntarily protects Miss Crane from rioters after she remarks, "it's me they want" (J 55). On each occasion the Indian is killed and the Anglo-Indians hasten away (running, in a car, on a train). However, while Miss Crane returns to Mr. Chaudhuri's side to clasp his hand, it is not Sarah but Guy Perron who returns to the side of Ahmed's dead body, and it is Guy's living hand that is steadied by Sarah as they both tremble after their ordeal (D 590).

Scott leaves his fiction with this incident, having returned full-circle to his starting-point and highlighted variations between the two sets of events that are implied by the historical significance of the intervening years. The woman running from the violence of the Bibighar that stemmed from her relationship with an Indian has widened into the raj fleeing from the horror of mass murder and rioting throughout India. From the perspective of the final volume, Scott's narrator can see the ties that bind all these events together, the links that couple places and times. While on another rail journey, the narrator recalls Ahmed Kasim's death: "Increasing speed, the train puts distance between itself and the falling body and between one time and another" (D 112). Ahmed's murder is the culmination of Scott's reconstruction of the last years of the raj, and consequently Ahmed's body "will not fall to the ground so much as out of a history which began with a girl stumbling on steps at the end of a long journey through the dark" (D 113). The narrator is emphasizing the importance of an event which happened five years before and many miles away because he sees the situation in August 1947 in terms of a history which began on the first page of the *Quartet*.[22]

The image of Daphne running has suggested these other images and several more in the course of the tetralogy. Consequently, it is important to note that most images are the product of going in through the back of another, of exploring the situation from another perspective. For example, Scott explains in one of his essays how images of Miss Crane, such as the one of her sitting by the roadside holding Mr. Chaudhuri's hand, derived from the image of Daphne running, because they were all pictures of Anglo-Indians outside of the "closed safe little circle" of their own kind (M 66). Again, this suggests that it is by taking a spatial reading of all the text together that an understanding of Scott's arrangement of the *Quartet* is possible.

As Robert Scholes once asserted, "one must, as a critic, move back and forth between theory and history, between idea and fact" (ix). It is similarly necessary to follow this precept by moving from Scott's historical perspective to his fictional theory and practice. In the rest of this study, I will also move between history and theory in order to demonstrate how Scott deploys and questions "facts," and to show that, in the *Quartet* as elsewhere, there is never just *an* idea but always ideas in dialogue. While this study is not written from a post-colonial perspective, the attention to plurality, hybridity, and dialogue in recent essays by Bill Schwarz and Danny Colwell has shown that the *Quartet* ought to be seen as a sustained exercise in colonial critique in terms of both content and form.[23] By contrast, readings which confine Scott's work to the "raj nostalgia" of the early 1980s or the familiar tropes of imperial psychic drives that he sought to expose and undermine by working through, seem themselves complicit with attempts to keep in place the stereotypes of empire. My intention here is to show how the "situation" looked to one writer in the 1960s and early 1970s, prior to the publication of Edward Said's *Orientalism* and in the midst of the liberal crisis that had followed from an imperial collapse—when the British had "come to the end of themselves."

CHAPTER ONE

Colonial Narrative:
Geography and Mystery

Any British novel set in India immediately concerns itself with the large
history of fiction about colonialism. The *Quartet* must be considered to
be in dialogue with those other texts and particularly with *A Passage to
India*, which Scott wrote about on several occasions.[1]

A comparison arises between the *Quartet* and *A Passage to India* not
least because, in Western literary terms, Forster's novel, more than *Kim*,
has become *the* story about India under the raj. Richard Cronin, for
example, expresses a sentiment that he imagines many others share:
"before I ever went there, India already existed for me, existed completely. . . . India had been given to me by E. M. Forster" (177). There
are also structural and thematic links. In addition to the pivotal device of
an alleged rape, the novels share suggestions of homo-eroticism between Merrick and Hari on the one hand and Fielding and Aziz on the
other.[2] There is also Barbie's telepathy and Mrs. Moore's, coupled with
their loss of a connection with God (after visiting the Marabar cave Mrs.
Moore "didn't want to communicate with anyone, not even with God"
[146]); the interest in the Amritsar incident, which shocked both
authors deeply;[3] the use of "repetition with variation," which Forster
termed "rhythm" and Scott called "going in through the back of the
image"; a possibly similar use of India as body and England as soul
(Weinbaum 1981); and finally an emphasis on the barriers to union
or friendship that stand between countries and individuals. The two
writers' allegiance to liberal humanism also suggests a link, yet Scott
denied any direct influence from Forster on his work (Spurling 375),
and this makes it the more important to see whether Scott presents a
different view of India and Anglo-India.

To begin with, while Forster and Scott both use accusations of rape as
catalytic events in their novels, they do so for different reasons.[4] The
narrative purposes of the alleged rapes in *A Passage to India* and *The Jewel
in the Crown* diverge in the following ways. Adela's (self-)assault—which
is literally non-existent in Forster's published novel but present in the
original manuscript—is depicted as a rude awakening from her dream

of a quest for the "real" India. She has her English calm ruffled by India's hot climate and unfamiliar people, which is to say that her bewilderment is engendered by her ignorance of the country and the customs she has encountered. This is a common "English" theme Forster has already used with respect to the clash between English sensibilities and what he saw as Italian passion in *A Room with a View* and *Where Angels Fear to Tread*. For Scott, Daphne's rape, together with the synchronous imprisonments and reprisals around Mayapore, is symptomatic of the history of Britain's occupation of India. And, as I have already suggested, that an English woman, not an Indian woman, is raped is an example of Scott's exploring the back of the image (as is Merrick's sexual abuse of Hari, which Scott presents as the main microcosmic image of Britain's rape of India). This is made explicit by Daphne's comparison, much more common in earlier drafts of *The Jewel in the Crown*, between her rape and that of India: "There is that old, disreputable saying, isn't there? 'When rape is inevitable, lie back and enjoy it.' *Well, there has been more than one rape.* I can't say, Auntie, that I lay back and enjoyed mine. But Lili was trying to lie back and enjoy what we've done to her country" (J 434). In Forster's text, the rape is part of a spiritual design: "*A Passage to India* . . . passes beyond humanistic morality to a basically metaphysical critique of man's fate . . . its main point is that God's will, if it exists at all, cannot be known in human terms" (Crews 88). Instead, Scott provides an historical and political image of events that happened in 1857, 1919, and 1942 (even Brigadier Reid makes a comparison between these dates [J 278]).[5] Scott wishes to show that even selfless feelings are insufficient to transcend the reality of colonialism—the imperial embrace has always resulted in violence. There is present throughout *A Passage to India* the suggestion that Adela's desire to know Indians is not much more than a puzzled inquisitiveness, whereas Scott uses a character whose genuine and sincere love is insufficient against the resentment, prejudice, aggression, and division that have come to exist between Briton and Indian. Scott also ends *The Jewel in the Crown* with an extended insight into Daphne's feelings and perspective, whereas Forster not only inserts a caesura for Adela's experience but then distances her from the main narrative.

While Forster's 1924 novel, begun and set pre-war, ends with hope for the British-Indian future, Scott's novel ensures that the colonial animus doesn't end with Independence and shows it clearly at his time of writing, through the narrator's personal experience. Here, Scott makes two points. First, that friendship should not be shown to be broken by the intrusion of the Indian landscape (and even Orwell's

Burmese Days suggests this in the earthquake that separates Flory and Elizabeth just before he proposes to her) but by the racism fostered by legal, political, and social discrimination. Secondly, that colonial practices continue beyond colonialism, because behind them there persists a prejudice built on ignorance and inherited assumptions of Caucasian racial ascendancy (in which Merrick explicitly says he believes [S 217]). Its persistence results in calls for immigration clampdowns, the need to implement "Race" laws, and the shift to a burgeoning cultural imperialism.[6]

India, according to Scott, was a subject most English people thought none of their concern and felt had been summed up in literature by 1924: "the subject is thought to have been dealt with satisfactorily enough by the late E. M. Forster in his novel *A Passage to India*" (M 112). Yet, for many critics, Forster had in several ways established a collective Indian stereotype. This is Nirad Chaudhuri's argument against Godbole, "a clown," and Aziz, who is, Forster says, "like most Orientals."[7] Chaudhuri concludes that Forster trivializes Indian suffering under imperial rule through his refusal to treat it seriously in the novel. Forster sees Indians as representative rather than individual. As Said writes, "Orientalism is never far from what Denys Hay has called the Idea of Europe, a collective notion identifying 'us' Europeans as against all 'those' non-Europeans . . ." (*Orientalism* 7). In *A Passage to India*, both Godbole and Aziz are representatively different.

Scott addresses this problem by mixing English class discrimination with colonial racism. Issues of class and race are intertwined, and Scott, with contemporary critics such as Benedict Anderson, understands the latter as analogous to an extreme example of the former (149). Unlike class, however, racism had been an issue rarely addressed seriously by Western capitalism or socialism. According to Scott this was because Europe had been exclusively concerned with its own struggles and had been ignorant of the history and civilization of the Other, attitudes that allowed the West initially to define itself as an area of confrontation as well as to enjoy a high level of material comfort. Hélène Cixous's comments seem entirely appropriate here:

> With the dreadful simplicity that orders the movement Hegel erected as a system, society trots along before my eyes reproducing to perfection the mechanism of the death struggle: the reduction of a "person" to the position of "other"—the inexorable plot of racism. There has to be some "other"—no master without a slave, no economico-political power without exploitation, no dominant class without cattle under the yoke, no "Frenchmen" without wogs, no Nazis without Jews. . . . (*The Newly Born Woman*, qtd. Young 2-3)

27

Forster, though presenting Indian stereotypes at one level, believed strongly in eroding the differences between individuals and in working against "the inexorable plot of racism"; and this is a major point of contact between his liberal humanism and Scott's. Each was appalled by the corruption of personal relationships brought about by imperial rule. The inability to connect is shown in both writers by the insularity of the British, the invisibility of Indians to Anglo-Indians, and the divisions created within even the British community by its rule. Hence, Fielding's ostracism from the Club, Mrs. Moore's loss of patience, and Adela's on-off engagement. Cyril Connolly, in his *Enemies of Promise* (1938), from which Scott frequently quoted, says, "the novels of Forster state the general conflict which is localised in the political conflict of today. His themes are the breaking down of barriers: between white and black, between class and class, between man and woman, between art and life. 'Only connect . . . ,' the motto of *Howard's End*, might be the lesson of all his work" (18). Despite this, a number of criticisms have been levelled at Forster by critics such as Chaudhuri and Suleri. For instance, there are undoubtedly generalizations about Indians made by the narrator of *A Passage to India* that are for the most part unmatched by similar observations on (all) the British: "like all Indians, [Aziz] was skilful in the slighter impertinences" (271). Remarks such as this build up the impression that Forster is writing to "us" about "them."

The self/other distinction of course runs deep and is often considered, by Freud and Bakhtin for example, to be embedded in the individual as well as society.[8] Scott sees the self split between its conscious side and its hidden side, which he describes in terms of an image from Lorca, of the *duende*: "a little black hunchback who draws pictures on the walls of his dungeon. When I find the pictures moving he shrieks with laughter. When I find them comic I hear him weeping in the straw" (C 117).[9] In the *Quartet* this is present in the discrepancy between characters such as Lady Manners and Sarah on the one hand, and Merrick and Hari on the other ("On Kumar's part a darkness of the soul. On Merrick's a darkness of the mind and heart and flesh" [J 144]). Scott broadens this picture of the divided self to include India and the raj. As we will see, division in and between people at all levels is of primary concern to him, and he uses it as a symbol of the division of the sub-continent that "crowned" the failure to unify India in approximately 150 years of British rule.

The link between the physical and the metaphysical appears regularly in colonial fiction, and the most obvious way in which novels construct the West's Other is through geography, which is often then transferred to a metaphysical dimension. Scott deplored this tendency, as he made clear in a review:

> The publisher's description of Ved Mehta's *Portrait of India* as "the first [*sic*] definitive book on present-day India and likely to be historic in its singular power to make India, at last, real and comprehensible to Western readers," is a striking example of the compulsion to reach the heart of an imaginary darkness, a compulsion further aggravated by a hidden grievance: a suspicion that the Indians must have access to spiritual resources which enable them to survive in conditions that would kill any ordinary people off. Never having found India either unreal or incomprehensible I cannot say whether Mr. Mehta's book will help to make it less so.[10]

And this proclivity extends to informed and perceptive critics also. For example, Goonetilleke, considering the picaresque form of *Kim*, cites approvingly Richard Schechner, who observed, "Ramayana, after all, literally means the goings of Rama. The idea of a processional movement is very important in India. India is a geometaphysical place" (52). This is certainly true to the picture painted by much colonial fiction, and not only of India. *Kim, Heart of Darkness*, and *A Passage to India* are all stories of travel, and each concerns itself with a metaphysical journey as well as a geographical one: on the "Wheel of Life," into the layers of kinship with the primitive self beneath "civilized" behaviour, and towards the "twilight of the double vision," as Forster has it (193).

But how is the importance of a geographical difference between East and West arrived at? Said, indebted to Saussure's argument of definition through difference, of language as a system with no positive terms, states,

> [The Orient] is not merely *there*, just as the Occident is not just *there* either. We must take seriously Vico's comment that men make their own history, that what they can know is what they have made, and extend it to geography: as both geographical and cultural entities—to say nothing of historical entities—such locales, regions, geographical sectors as "Orient" and "Occident" are man-made. (*Orientalism* 4-5)

Sara Suleri, perhaps thinking of analogies with the map in *King Solomon's Mines* or Colonel Creighton's Indian survey in *Kim*, characterizes colonial fiction's treatment of geography in this way:

> Typically, the narrator is a cartographer, the only locus of rationality in an area of engulfing unreliability, so that ultimately the narrative mind is the only safe terrain the texts provide. India itself, like a Cheshire cat, functions as a dislocated metaphor for an entity that is notoriously remiss in arriving at

the appointed place at the correct time. As a consequence, it becomes a space that imposes its unreality on western discourse to the point where the narrative has no option but to redouble on itself, to internalize the symbolic landscape of India in order to make it human. Thus geography is subsumed into the more immediate and familiar territory of the liberal imagination, in the act of recolonizing its vagrant subject with the intricacies of a defined sensibility. Such is the imagination, of course, that legitimizes a text like *A Passage to India* as a humanely liberal parable of imperialism, and allows a reader like Trilling to interpret the novel's depiction of Eastern action as a metaphor for the behaviour of the West. In other words, the only difference of India inheres in the fact that it is symbolic of something the western mind must learn about itself.[11]

Suleri argues that, in the use of metaphoric geography, the West's Others most often appear, as in Naipaul's *An Area of Darkness*, as unfathomable holes, spaces, lacunae, places uninhabited by "civilized" people, God, or Western morality: "Forster . . . constructs a symbolic geography that provides western narrative with its most compelling and durable image of India, which is, of course, the figure of India as a hollow, or a cave" (246). This corresponds with other faults (muddle, contradiction) that Forster attributes to India whether in the space of Cave, Temple, or Mosque. However, Suleri's stress on hollows fails to emphasize the Christian element of *A Passage to India*; the Jain caves of the middle section are also symbolic of Western spiritual vacancy, sandwiched between the holy buildings of a Muslim Mosque and a Hindu Temple, where the Christian Church ought to reside. Suleri's argument also seems at odds with much of Forster's presentation of infinity and boundlessness—of the overarching sky, the circles of people that no earthly invitation can embrace, the silence beyond the remotest echo. The small spaces in the novel are more often the places resorted to by the English body and mind unable to cope without limitations. It is the openness that tires the "souls" of Forster's characters, Indian and British, and encourages them to retreat "to the permanent lines which habit or chance have dictated" (225).

The characterization of India as a place without bounds complements Forster's inscription of it as an inexplicable place without rationality: "Hassan . . . found it possible not to hear him; heard and didn't hear, just as Aziz had called and hadn't called. 'That's India all over . . . how like us . . . there we are'" (104). This is in fact little more than an extension of Cromer's view, popular in Europe, that logic is ignored by "the Oriental."[12]

In Forster's metaphoric system it is also the topography of India which keeps East and West necessarily apart (in other words it defines their limits), and prevents the embrace which, by contrast, Scott sees as characterizing the British hold on India. Suleri writes,

Finally, what prevents the European and the Indian from completing their embrace is the obliterating presence of the landscape. The European wants the completion of his desire in the present moment, yet the narrative gives the last word to the land's great power to deny and disappear. (249-50)

The importance of geography ultimately lies in its crude definition of East and West and the people found in each. For the Europeans, alien soil becomes a metaphor for those who live on it, and the West's response to the land is a correlative of its response to these "non-Europeans." At the end of T. E. Lawrence's work, for example,

we are left with a sense of the pathetic distance still separating "us" from an Orient destined to bear its foreignness as a mark of its permanent estrangement from the West. This is the disappointing conclusion corroborated (contemporaneously) by the ending of E. M. Forster's *A Passage to India*, where Aziz and Fielding attempt, and fail at, reconciliation.

(Said, *Orientalism* 244)

For Scott, this distance becomes indicative of the difference not between West and East, but between Anglo-Indians and "the people [they] really are," the Britons at home. It remains a cultural symbol, but one of the difference between the "exile" and the people the exile "belongs" to. This is most fully developed in the character of Sarah Layton who is constantly aware that "The English who went to India were different from those who didn't" (S 77). But Scott's difference from Forster is also there in the originating image of the *Quartet*, of Daphne running. She is not, like Adela, an example of the European running from a side of herself she has had first to journey away from the West to find. Instead, in Scott's words, she is a person "who, falling in love with an Indian, attempted to associate with him simply as a human being. When it comes to it . . . we find that she is running to *save* that association, *not running away from it*" (M 68).

A further difference between Scott and Forster lies in their attitudes towards what the latter would call muddle. Said, on British writers of Orientalist works, including Byron, George Eliot,[13] T. E. Lawrence, and Forster, argues that "All these writers give a bolder outline to Disraeli's 'great Asiatic mystery'" (Said, *Orientalism* 99). So, Forster repeatedly presents Indians as peculiar: "they did not one thing which the non-

31

Hindu would feel dramatically correct; this approaching triumph of India was a muddle (as we call it), a frustration of reason and form" (258). That this sense of muddle and mystery cultivated by Forster and often seen as one of *A Passage to India*'s strengths is not found in Scott's tetralogy can be construed as a poetic difference. Forster's enigmatic style tends towards mystification and obfuscation, whereas Scott's more concrete style avoids such an otherworldly feel—a trait some critics find debilitating: "untouched by the poetry which animates Forster's work . . . this [is an] essayist's prose" (Walsh 174-75). For Forster, the mystery is justified precisely because he is writing about India:

> In the cave it is *either* a man, *or* the supernatural, *or* an illusion. If I say, it becomes whatever the answer a different book. And even if I know! My writing mind therefore is a blur here—i.e. I will it to remain a blur, and to be uncertain, as I am of many facts in daily life. This isn't a philosophy of aesthetics. *It's a particular trick I felt justified in trying because my theme was India.* It sprang straight from my subject matter. I wouldn't have attempted it in other countries, which though they contain mysteries or muddles, manage to draw rings round them.[14]

Even if it is argued that Forster's main point is not about India but concerns existential uncertainty, as he has intimated by saying "I tried to indicate the human predicament in a universe which is not, so far, comprehensible to our minds,"[15] then it is still enormously significant that he felt justified in using India, not England or a Mediterranean country, for this purpose. Forster's is also a paradoxical method in which an environment alien to the novelist and the West is used to designate mystery while the created confusion is then used to define that same environment.

Scott, in contrast to Forster's utilization of the mystery of the Marabar Caves to express India, uses versions of the Bibighar Affair (as it comes to be known, in the same way that the Jallianwallah Bagh massacre of 1919 is sometimes called the Amritsar Incident) to make problematic any individual account of an event. Scott is concerned less with what happened than with the ways in which people decide to explain what happened and use those explanations for political ends.

Throughout Scott's novels, the British disgust at "muddle" is seen as a part of their own desire for hierarchy; Lili Chatterjee says the British "divide the material from the spiritual with their usual passion for tidiness and for people being orderly and knowing their place" (J 66). In Forster's novel, the mystery is another form of stating the lack of logic and rational order in India, which is the habitual Western response:

"Accuracy is abhorrent to the Oriental mind. Every Anglo-Indian should always remember that maxim."[16] And this mystery which is ascribed to other people will inevitably be used against them in considerations of honesty, humanity, and good and evil.

For Forster, everything in India is either a confusion or a paradox. For example, his narrator, using characteristically enigmatic words, tells us in the "Temple" section that the god, and other offerings thrown into the river, were "emblems of passage; a passage not easy, not now, not here, not to be apprehended except when it is unattainable" (283). The chief exponent of this "Oriental logic" is Godbole, who says at one point, "everything is anything and nothing something" (169), and who is privileged with preternatural powers, with a "telepathic appeal" which links him with Mrs. Moore. In Scott's *Quartet* the same can be said for Barbie Batchelor, and yet the point being made is entirely different. For Scott, his character's ability is to represent and to predict: Barbie is on the one hand an illustrative figure who embodies a view of history that Scott adopts from Emerson, and on the other hand a person who, even if unconsciously, perceives historical forces which will shape the future. For Forster, however, telepathy is another piece of mystification predicated on his personal experience, about which he comments at one point in *The Hill of Devi*: "it is not the only time that I have wondered whether the Maharajah might possess super-normal faculties" (87).

Scott avoids this obfuscation by refusing to see India in metaphysical terms, an approach that Walsh sees as a fault: "Religion of every sort is not, it appears[,] something Scott understands or can realize in fiction —a severe handicap for one dealing with an essentially spiritual universe" (Walsh 177). By painting a political and historical portrait of the raj, Scott avoids the common Western flirtation with Indian religion and refuses either to employ metaphysics as another index of difference or to divert attention from the material aspects of Britain's presence in India. Finally, it is important to remember that spiritual strength was part of the argument for Britain's right to rule at all, and as such was applied to Britain's moral leadership of the world. It was a reason for commanding loyalty which Gandhi at least found convincing. In August 1914, he believed that Britain had "an Empire founded not on material but on spiritual foundations" (qtd. Huttenback 109).

In contrast with Forster, by foregrounding politics in his presentation of imperialism, Scott is engaging with the main material elements of the raj and not obscuring physical colonial relationships behind metaphysical speculations. The *Quartet* is undeniably more about the raj and its rule, administration, and treatment of India, than about India's experience under the raj. As such it is a book about failure, but not about the failure Suleri identifies for Western fictions set in India:

> From *A Passage to India* on, "books about India" have been more accurately books about the representation of India, with each offering variants of the peculiar logic through which a failure of representation becomes transformed into a characteristically Indian failure.   (245)

While the *Quartet* can be said to be a book about the pictorial and political representation of India, in Scott's novels the failure is an English one, and it is the purpose of the *Quartet* to demonstrate the failure necessitated by an ingrained racism which is not characteristic of the raj so much as the way the West's meeting with its Others has evolved race as the primary signifier of status, before class, gender, religion, or nationality.

CHAPTER TWO

Exile and the Fall of Empire

Having identified Scott as an author more interested in social and historical issues than metaphysical ones, I will now discuss his use of themes and images derived from religious history. In particular, Scott portrays the decline of the raj in terms of variations on the Judaeo-Christian myths of Eden, the Fall, and the loss of paradise.[1]

Scott's utilization of seminal themes from biblical stories, particularly Genesis, has its basis in the Western belief in a religious justification to the imperial project, seeing colonialism as moral expansionism, as dutiful crusade. Scott therefore employs parallels with the myth of the Fall to suggest not the spiritual emptiness of India but the downfall of British self-belief and self-righteousness. For Anglo-Indians in the *Quartet* this collapse is worsened by the gulf between the raj and Britain. Here, Scott introduces the theme of exile which he exploits in its postlapsarian context and in its simple meaning of a prolonged absence from one's home or country. He is particularly interested in the effects of exile on a people he considers to be characterized by insularity. As an opening example of the pains of exile, there is this lament:

> Persons who have never quitted their native land, cannot imagine the passionate regrets experienced by the exile, who in the midst of the most gorgeous scenes pines after the humblest objects surrounding that home to which he dares not hope to return . . . where all is strange, the very magnificence of the landscape is apt to revolt the mind, and many persons will . . . contrast the Ganges with some obscure rivulet, the magnolia with the daisy, to the disparagement of the mighty river and the monarch of flowers. To do justice to the sunny land of India, its visitors should have the power to leave it for Europe at pleasure. . . .[2]

This sense of melancholy lingers over all the Anglo-Indians in Scott's novels, but it is exacerbated by the realization that they are also dying in exile. This occurs most strongly in Sarah, who thinks of herself belonging to a fallen world in which she has inherited the empty shell of "that extinction-through-exile that awaited Muirs and Laytons and all their kind" (S 431).[3] At the end of the *Quartet* the raj is left, just days before Independence, awaiting only the official ceremony of the transfer of power.

35

The first book of *The Day of the Scorpion* is called "The Prisoners in the Fort." The fort is used as an image of the prejudice and fear common to strangers in an alien land. Its walls represent a kind of isolationism practised by a racial coterie in its strict exclusion of outsiders. Scott wrote in a draft of *The Towers of Silence*:

> "And their lives are somehow second-hand," Barbie informed God that night. "Here of course we are all exiles from our native heath and unless we are careful we become like little fortresses, bristling with prejudices." [4]

The British in India, for Scott, embodied traits, beliefs, and shared characteristics unlike those of the British "at home," unexposed to alien cultures and foreign climates. Because they were exiles, their shared sense of being British meant far more to the enclaves in India than it did to the UK population.

Post-war Britain, for the first time in over two hundred years, was only a moderate international power in economic decline, its imperial status having decisively shifted to the superpowers of the Cold War. Radical social legislation reflected the changes of principle throughout a war-torn Europe in which a policy of "liberation" superseded an imperial tradition that in some quarters was being placed on the same moral level as *lebensraum*. So, in the *Quartet*, while Barbie Batchelor explains that she can no longer remember what her principles are, Nigel Rowan can see his partly treacherous work with the Princely States at the time of Independence in terms of liberty—as an Emersonian "triumph of principles" (D 498). Because India was freed through the parliamentary process and not as a direct consequence of armed struggle, the *Quartet* probes both how the British "lost" their Empire and how they quasi-suicidally "came to the end of themselves" (a *felo de se* represented in the deaths of Teddie, Merrick, Barbie, Miss Crane and others). This is a phrase which Scott uses on several occasions in his fiction, and yet the only place he explains it in any detail is in an unused script for a proposed television interview with Melvyn Bragg. For this reason, the interview is worth quoting at length:

> Bragg: What does the English "came to the end of themselves" mean? And why particularly in India?
>
> Scott: Not in India only. For me, metaphorically, yes. When I write about the India of the raj, as I do, I'm using it, always have used it, as a metaphor. Walter Allen described the novel as an extended metaphor of its author's view of life. India is my extended metaphor. I write about it, as accurately as I can, but it is always a metaphor. . . . The easy assumption is that one is writing out of regret, grief, for a lost greatness—the pomp and circumstance of which

36

these images are the lingering reminder. But that's not what I'm writing about. Sometimes the pomp creeps into the metaphor. [A modern young Indian in England] is in the metaphor. What is he? An immigrant? Or a young student at say the London School of Economics? His prospects, when he goes back to India, will be better than they were forty years ago. He might then, just have scraped into the provincial civil service, or even into the ICS. Today his expectations are higher, but he's more likely to be going back to become a junior executive in a firm manufacturing consumer products. More central to the metaphor is this [young English man]. What is he? A graduate from Essex or Warwick? What are his expectations? 40 years ago he might have been on his way to India, with the prospect of having in a few years 4000 square miles of territory under his executive and judicial power.

It was all wrong, of course. It was none of his business. I'm glad the job is no longer there for him to do. The young Indian will do it just as well. But being glad isn't the same as assuming to know that he would have done it badly. That he was inevitably going to be a Turton or a Burton. He would in all likelihood have done it very well. What he has to do well now is what puzzles me. Sell soapflakes? I look at this young man and see him as a member of a society which idealistically and properly divested itself of its colonial and imperial powers and then found itself naked—an emperor without clothes —exposed to the bitter winds of the mid 20th century—a society that gradually woke up to the fact that, apart from the daily routine of making something to sell so that you could buy what you needed, to survive, there seemed little else to put your mind to. A society without an ideology. A society that had come to the end of itself as it was. In India this end was especially poignant. There, they carried on right to the bitter end, doing the jobs that had been there to be done, no longer were. When we speak today of needing to do something about the quality of life (the verb used is usually "improve," as though a new product was on the market), when we talk about looking for a new role, going for growth but also for a new ideal, I can only nod. I hate the jargon, but know what is meant. I've been writing about it for years—the importance of a job to the man who does it. You could find many metaphors for this—my own is the Indian metaphor because, I suppose, I realised how dedicated the Turtons and Burtons really were, and also realised how great an opportunity India gave the average middle-class Englishman to extend himself. Not making money, but accepting responsibility for the welfare of thousands of people. The English have always been very insular. But also great adventurers. The Indians are just as insular, but great travellers. I see so much better what connects us than what divides us.[5]

Some of these sentiments, prompted by reflection on Britain's new place in the world, are reminiscent of Jimmy Porter's lament in *Look Back in Anger* that "there aren't any good, brave causes left" and of his grudging respect for Colonel Redfern who, though "left over from the

Edwardian wilderness" and unable to "understand why the sun isn't shining anymore," has, like Scott's characters, a sense of responsibility and a cause, whether good, bad, or indifferent, to work for (84, 66-67). This loss of a cause and a belief in the light of past glories marks Scott's characters apart from Forster's, and makes them never emissaries but always exiles. Scott wrote in one of his essays:

> My Turtons exist not in perpetual Edwardian sunshine, but in the shadows, the melancholy of exile. There are exceptions, but the lighting is thus, the climate so. They realize that they no longer swim boldly on the tide of affairs. The Edwardian sunlight that sometimes still seems to dapple the waters is an illusion and, by and large, they know it.   (M 126-27)

The illusion is caused by distance in time and space; the English warmth (as opposed to the heat of India) yields a glow stored in memory, exported when fresh, and never grown old: "in the colonial society established by the British in Benares, officials who made up the dominant class had gone out to India when young and with an idealized view of their own society and culture, an adolescent view which was arrested in India" (Parry 57). Scott thought that by the 1940s this view made them exiles from "their own people" in terms of belief, national self-image, and values. Sarah Layton sets up an opposition in her mind between the raj and the nation it represents, "the people we really are." It is only when she meets one of these people, Clark, that she is confirmed in her suspicion of the raj's emotional and mental distance from people back "home" in Britain:

> I was up in 'Pindi staying with a friend of a friend back home who's been out here for about ten years. And there they were, the man, the wife, and two of the po-faced kids, and right from the beginning we felt towards each other like I suppose those people who suffer from that odd racial prejudice thing, as if in spite of our being the *same* colour and class, one of us was black, me, and the others white, them. We were tremendously polite but simply had nothing to say to each other.   (S 426)

Sarah sympathizes with Clark to the extent that she feels that, had she been brought up exclusively in England, she would have shared many of his views, manners, and morals—but in India she feels neither like Clark nor like a "daughter of the raj." She is liminally placed, at the intersection of two worlds:

> Looking at Sarah Barbie felt she understood a little of the sense the girl might have of having no clearly defined world to inhabit, but one poised between the old for which she had been prepared, but which seemed to be

38

dying, and the new for which she had not been prepared at all. Young, fresh and intelligent, all the patterns to which she had been trained to conform were fading, and she was already conscious just from chance or casual encounter of the gulf between herself and the person she would have been if she had never come back to India: the kind of person she "really was."

(T 272)

Scott portrays this situation as something of a Fall—even if it is an inevitable one given the injustice of colonial rule—and he is concerned to chart the momentum of that descent in particular individuals. There are those who have found themselves, like Sarah, born into an unacceptable history, and those, like Barbie, who are still living out a history for which there is no longer any room and for which, as she says of her trunk, there is "no *use*" (T 273). Sarah feels intensely an incongruence between her private and public selves which undermines her sense of identity. Her distance from her own past mirrors both her distance from "home" and the distance she feels from the role that history has assigned to her.

To understand these aspects of the novels it is necessary to plot their co-ordinates, and one way that Scott encourages the reader to do this is through the religious iconography of the garden, the Fall, and subsequent exile.[6] He opens the second part of *The Jewel in the Crown* with this comparison: "Next, there is the image of a garden: not the Bibighar garden but the garden of the MacGregor House: intense sunlight, deep and complex shadows" (J 63). From this point on, this image represents a mixture of intense hope and crushing failure; it has associations of both home and eviction. To begin with, there are the significant gardens in the novels: the Bibighar Gardens, the MacGregor House gardens, Mayapore's Chillianwallah Bagh (bagh means "garden"), M. A. Kasim's garden at Premanagar fort, and the garden at Rose Cottage. All these gardens, or the people associated with them, have ominous pasts and uneasy futures.

Like the play of light and shadow in the quotation above, within the image of a garden there is inevitably a confrontation of cultivation and nature—or, more explicitly, a case of Western aesthetics of harmony and form, developed over the nineteenth century, imposed on small squares of the massive Indian landscape. The link between the Bibighar Gardens and the MacGregor House initiates a movement of the *Quartet*'s story into the past, with its violent embrace of Indians and British. To begin with, Scott's narrator, a traveller to India in 1964, tells us that the Bibighar Gardens and the MacGregor House and garden are haunted, and that the "first ghost" stands on the verandah where

Daphne collapsed after running from the Bibighar.[7] Next, he adds Daphne to the ghosts who "warn people with white skins that the MacGregor House is not a good place for them to be" (J 136). These spirits recall the historical dangers of mixing dark and light skins, passions, or personalities. How else can the narrator "account for the occasional sound of stoutly shod feet mounting the stairs or crossing the tiled floor of the main hall except by admitting Miss Manners's continued presence?" (J 71).[8] Thus, the events of the *Quartet* are seen as links in a chain of destroyed loves, and the individual events have to be taken as episodes in a historical series.

The history of the MacGregor House and garden, and their relation to the Bibighar, has two parts, the first of which concerns a late eighteenth-century prince who "conceived a passion for a singer of classical music" (J 64) and built for her a house on the site of the MacGregor House, as it is now known. This develops into a tale of, on the one hand, love never consummated, and, on the other, "love" for courtesans; of a people starved and a house deserted; of an Englishman killed and a state annexed. This part of the story is one of love that has failed to unite on any level. Most of the second part of the history of the garden, set in the nineteenth century, is told by Sister Ludmila, a Western woman who attempts like Daphne to connect across the barrier of race (she has established a "sanctuary" for the homeless and dying, providing "a clean bed, a hand to hold" [J 123]). Sister Ludmila tells not one but several versions of this part of the story (introducing a major component of the *Quartet*'s structure, competing narrative accounts). One version is described as European, while two others are Indian:

> You see how the facts about MacGregor do not fit the story that he burned the Bibighar because it was an abomination? But then this was the European version of the tale. Perhaps, also, it is the story he told his wife, whom he married and brought to Mayapore only after he had established his fortune and rebuilt the singer's house and called it by his own name. By that time he had already burned Bibighar, not, according to the Indian version, because it was an abomination in his eye and the eye of the Lord, an abomination even twenty or thirty years after its last occupation, but because he fell in love with an Indian girl and lost her to a boy whose skin was the same colour as her own. There are two versions of the Indian account of the burning of Bibighar. The first is that he discovered the girl and her lover met in the Bibighar, and that he then destroyed it in a fit of jealous rage. The second is that he told the girl she would have to leave the MacGregor House and live in the Bibighar. He took her there and showed her the repairs he had made to it and the furnishings and clothes he had bought for her comfort and

enjoyment. When she asked him why she must leave the MacGregor House he said: Because I am going to Calcutta to bring back an English wife. So that night she stole away with her true lover. When he found that she had gone he ordered the Bibighar to be burned to the ground, and then utterly obliterated.   (J 135)

The stories of the garden offer up unhappy lovers, betrayal, and retribution (e.g. MacGregor is killed by "mutinous sepoys"). Both Indian accounts show a reversion to racial homogeneity. And each story begins with a genuine love—the prince's for the singer, MacGregor's for an Indian girl, Daphne's for Hari—yet they are all spoiled and all climax in division and suffering. The cumulative message of the stories is that there is no new paradise to be found during the 200 years of the raj's rule. The versions of the Bibighar mimic the story of Eden, whose significance for Indians and Anglo-Indians is linked to Scott's perennial interest in the search for prelapsarian innocence. The warning of the garden in India only serves to strengthen the longing the raj has for Shakespeare's "other Eden, demi-paradise."

There are also several characters, such as Barbie, whose innocence is unknowingly lost in exile. They will never return to a half-forgotten world, preserved in memory, but will remain unaware that that world is now altered. Significantly, the awareness of loss is most strikingly present in an Indian. Philoctetes's eulogies mourn the passing of the elms and rooks of his youth, which are now replaced by palms and crows: "the familiar spirits of dead white sahibs and living black inheritors alike" (J 154). The success of Hari's indoctrination into English sentiment is present in his inheritance of such emotions about "home."

The gardens in the *Quartet* are fallen places—where lovers will break the rules of their environment, be punished, and come to the end of themselves as they are—but some are also redolent of Eden's peace and tranquillity. This is found by Mabel Layton in the "Eden" at Rose Cottage and for Kasim in his garden at Premanagar Fort.[9] Both gardens are to be short-lived and represent havens within the larger "prison" of Anglo-India (discussed in chapter 6).[10] While the Rose Cottage garden is turned into a tennis court, Kasim's garden is unremembered:

Here, in the courtyard, between August 1942 and the date of his release, the Fort's most distinguished prisoner created a garden to pass the time. Traces of it still remain. Given better luck . . . his memory might have been perpetuated by the habit, dear to Indians, of naming a place after its founder or its most illustrious inhabitant. But it is not known now as Kasim's Garden.

(S 5)

Only traces remain of Kasim's hope for Indian solidarity—his intention "to do the job that your Government has always found it beneficial to leave undone, the job of unifying India" (S 18). His hopeful vision is not realized in 1947 and, as though in consequence, there is no M. A. Kasim memorial garden at the Fort. Similarly, at Independence, Kasim's own family is both divided and bereaved. With partition, the dream of an undivided India has been broken, and the raj's loss of an English paradise will be felt also by Indians who hoped for unity and peace in a new, free land:

> "Kasim, I tell myself. Go and cultivate your garden for a while." He smiled.
>
> "At Premanagar I had plenty of practice." . . .
>
> "What have you in mind?"
>
> "At the moment only cultivating my garden. Doing everything I can to promote the claims of Fazal Huq Rahman and disputing the claims of Jinnah and his League for partition."   (D 443)

Everywhere in the *Quartet* gardens have troubled histories and futures. The raj has illusory visions of distant summer gardens and Kasim's attempt to cultivate a new united India is to end in bloodshed and division.

The garden, in its many forms in the *Quartet*, is symbolically linked for the raj with the Fall and exile of Adam and Eve (Hari and Daphne, and their forbidden love) and of Lucifer (Merrick and his sins of pride). However, Scott's image of the body falling is made explicit only in the final novel, *A Division of the Spoils*, where it is used as a correlative of the first image of the girl running. The narrator says that the falling body of Ahmed is explained by the story of the *Quartet*, "as if all that has gone before is explanation enough" (D 113).[11] That it is a Muslim who falls and not a member of the raj shows one way in which Scott is better able to see "what connects us than what divides us" and picks up the links between the Bible and the Koran. Like the relation between the stories of Miss Crane and Daphne, Ahmed's fall is a variation, "going in through the back of the image," on the theme of the fall of the raj. But it is one that also evokes the sense of an Indian fall from innocence (under a "God-like" foreign rule) into carnage and slaughter at Independence (the immediate responsibility of self-government). Scott does not trace a separate history for the different religious and national groups in the novels but blends them into one, fusing "the image of their separate destinies."

This fall is a question of history, in the sense that it is the direct consequence of a particular decision—Partition. The timing and method of Independence need not have been as they were, but once chosen—in a specific historical context—they was determining, irreversible decisions. In the *Quartet*, Merrick refuses to accept any inherited moral obligation from history, and Barbie, despite her occasional prophetic insights, cannot see how she is explained at all—cannot perceive the parallels between herself and history. Ahmed, however, understands his fall as the consequence of the history related in the *Quartet*:

> The victim chose neither the time nor the place of his death but in going to it as he did he must have seen that he contributed something of his own to its manner; and this was probably his compensation; so that when the body falls it will seem to do so without protest and without asking for any explanation of the thing that has happened to it, as if all that has gone before is explanation enough, so that it will not fall to the ground so much as out of a history that began with a girl stumbling on steps at the end of a long journey through the dark. (D 113)

Although this is the first explicit reference to the fall which results from the history of intolerance and violence demonstrated at Mayapore, images of falling have often occurred before. For example, the various sorts of "tower" of the third volume are falling and journeys are usually descents. For Barbie, these are watched over by God:

> [Mabel] twisted round as if to tell the tonga wallah to go back . . . that the time hadn't yet come and that the journey downhill must be cancelled, or anyway postponed. . . . God, [Barbie] felt, had waited a long time for her to see she could ignore the burden of her words which mounted one upon the other until they toppled, only to be set up again, and again, weighting her shoulders . . . as the equipage, avoiding the bazaar, dropped down.
> (T 183-84)

Falling, partly because of its biblical association with eviction, is linked in the *Quartet* with travelling, as in the passage above. The disaster precipitated by the over-hasty decolonization of India is echoed in Barbie's ill-thought-out decision finally to remove her trunk from Rose cottage.[12] Here there are associations of guilt, sin, and responsibility overlaid on images of colonial exile, migrations between India and Pakistan, and most particularly the departure of the raj. Thus, there are several descriptions of characters moving off and away in a guilty flight from an ugly scene, sometimes frenzied and sometimes invidiously calm: "Just then the engine driver up ahead obeyed an instruction and the train glided forward. It was the smooth gliding away from a violent

43

situation which one witness never forgot. 'Suddenly you had the feeling that the train, the wheels, the lines, weren't made of metal but of something greasy and evasive'" (D 112). It is not surprising, given Scott's shaping of history, examined in the next chapter, that the movement "away from a violent situation" has happened before: Daphne leaves such a situation on foot, Sarah and Guy by train, and the British by sea or air. With each variation Scott explores a new side of the same image to produce a different effect. The striking parallel, as suggested above, is with the British sliding away from India—because their iron grip and their sense of superiority have become greasier and looser as fresh doubts brush against them. The example of Edwina Crane illustrates how history is allegorized in the life of an individual. Miss Crane is famed for having resisted insurrection, for having stood firm under siege from "rebellious" Indians, echoing British stories of the sepoy uprising of 1857. Now, on a second occasion of unrest, in 1942, Miss Crane takes the decision to try to avoid confrontation by quitting her position; she travels with Mr. Chaudhuri but leaves him at his insistence (like the British quitting India), escaping by car. While Miss Crane is only abused, Mr. Chaudhuri is killed by his fellow Indians. Miss Crane continues her journey briefly, fleeing the violence, but returns, like those who later return to Ahmed's body, to realize that her concern comes "too late" and that her indecision and hasty flight have led to Mr. Chaudhuri's death.[13] Though she has not performed the killing, Miss Crane's profound awareness of direct responsibility is what Scott asks the British to feel with regard to all India after Independence.

So, the result of Scott's key epsiodes is always violence and death, and the circumstances are always those of travel. This mimics the peripatetic life of the exile and the Muslims, Hindus, and Anglo-Indians who were forced to move to new homes, to fall out of a long history into an uncertain future under new governments in Pakistan, India, and Britain. Near the start of the final novel, the narrator returns to the scene of Ahmed's murder:

> The train is cautious in its approach to Premanagar. Tracks converge from the east, coming from Mayapore. To the left, some miles distant, is the fort, no longer a prison, infrequently visited by tourists; peripheral to the tale, but a brooding point of reference and orientation. To the south, now, lies Mirat with its mosques and minarets. North, a few hours journey, is Ranpur, where a grave was undug, and farther north still, amid hills, Pankot, where it was dug in too great a hurry for someone's peace of mind. Beyond the fort, the west lies open, admitting a chill draft. The erosive wind, perhaps.   (D 113)

As indicated by this prolepsis of the end of the *Quartet*, Scott closes his story both at the centre of his fiction and at the centre of his images. This requires us to see Ahmed's "fall" as the necessary conclusion of the image of the girl running. From the east come tracks from Mayapore, the first novel, bringing the violence and intolerance of the Bibighar Affair. To the west is the fort, the "brooding point of reference and orientation" from the second novel, which signifies imprisonment no longer. To the north are the sites of the Laytons' experience of India and the towers of the third novel where Barbie saw the carrion crows and "sketched a point of reference. A minaret" (T 388). Lastly, to the south is Mirat, the princely state where a wedding and a stone rippled the surface of British society and where the principal characters gather once more at the end of *A Division of the Spoils*. At the centre is the train where the "chill draft" of God's breath—as will be discussed below—blows across a dark landscape on which thousands have been collectively sacrificed. It is a breath which blows higher the flames of riots and hatred. The bloodshed is a "fall" for India, but the raj has played the catalytic part of the serpent (Merrick is associated with the snake, and so is Hari by virtue of his pseudonym, Philoctetes). Independence is partly seen as a liberation from a tyrannical god, but it is also both a spoilage of Indian hopes for a peaceful, united country and an exposure of British principles, since Indian disharmony not only persists after two centuries of the raj but is exacerbated by Partition.

After the fall comes exile, a condition most fully realised in and by Sarah Layton. Early on she divests herself of the view of a divinely-appointed raj: "I look up and see that heaven is empty and that this is an age when all of us share the knowledge that it is and that there has never been a god nor any man made in that image" (S 213). Instead, her post-lapsarian question of identity is a psychological one that Sarah considers in terms of the raj's difference from the English at "home" and the effect of perpetual exile:

> It was a survival of exiles. Their enemy was light, not dark, the light of their own kind, of their own people at home from whom they had been too long cut off so that, returning there briefly, a deep and holy silence wrapped them and caused them to observe what was real as miniature. In India they had been betrayed by an illusion of topographical vastness into sins of pride that were foreign to their insular, pygmy natures. (S 404-05)

A young woman of Sarah's background is supposed to feel superior and elevated, but instead she feels false and marginal; like Eve after biting the apple she has knowledge of the world she inhabits and feels the stern, over-protective and therefore repressive paternalism of its rulers. She is doubly exiled because, while she is cut off with the other members of the raj, she also feels herself to be on their periphery. Her sense of a social presence is of an exilic liminality in which she is uncomfortable with her family in the closed circle of Anglo-India, but she is also distant from and unfamiliar with those she feels she resembles in Britain.

This last aspect to Sarah's view of Anglo-Indian identity connotes the impending demise of the raj and its precarious marginality—almost as though it were about to fall off the edge of the Empire rather than return to the centre. As a factor, marginality is most important in constructing identity because its very existence is not physical but mental, as is also the case for colonized peoples: "The 'marginal' and the 'central' are of course psychological constructs, but they have their grounding in the alienation resulting from colonial incorporation" (Ashcroft et al., 104). Their grounding can also lie in the charade of colonial service (the issues of charade and marginality come out strongly in *A Division of the Spoils* in the number of sexual and sartorial subversions Scott includes—Sophie Dixon, the transvestites at the Maharanee's party, Pinky, and, of course, Merrick). Sarah Layton's view of herself and the raj is of a hazy, unreal, peripheral existence of characters in a drama. This sensation is reinforced by the raj's marriage of hierarchy and solidarity:

> [Miss Crane] had few friends and still felt isolated from people as individuals, but she was aware now of a sense of community. . . . [I]ndifferently as Mrs. Nesbitt-Smith might sometimes treat her, Mrs. Nesbitt-Smith and her like would always rally round if she found herself in any kind of danger from outside the charmed circle of privilege on whose periphery she spent her days. (J 7)

These feelings of periphery and unreality are part of a more general feeling of not belonging, of having no home because "home" is not the place in which one has always lived, yet one can feel at home nowhere else. The most common example of this in literature is the exile's alienation and consequent aggression, which Benita Parry notes with regard to *A Passage to India*:

> While profiting from the fear on which the raj rests, the Anglo-Indians are victims of a fear which India nourishes in them. They live amidst scenery they do not understand, sense that Indians hate them and feel India to be a poisonous country intending evil against them. Already coarsened by their status in India, the crisis generated by Adela Quested's accusation against

Aziz hurls them into cruder demonstrations of their hostility, some demanding holocausts of natives, others longing to inflict humiliating punishment.

(Parry 279-80)

The striking mixture of animosity and guilt is present in the behaviour of many characters in the *Quartet* ranging from Merrick in Mayapore to the memsahibs in Pankot, and it is represented by the image of the fort I looked at earlier. But it is accentuated by an ever-decreasing sense of belonging. In a draft of *The Towers of Silence*, Scott illustrates how Barbie understands the legacy of General Dyer's massacre of Indians at Amritsar:

In 1919, Mrs. Fosdick, we wouldn't have stood for that sort of thing at home. Public whipping went out of fashion in the eighteenth century. And it's no good stopping up your ears Mrs. Smalley. In 1919 women like us went to *watch* it happen and jeered when the poor man screamed. You are much too young, but I anyway could easily have been among them. If I put myself in an Indian woman's shoes, then I have to wonder, I mean as I walk in the streets of Ranpur or the bazaar in Pankot, whether an Indian woman of my own age seeing me thinks: There goes one of the white memsahibs who probably laughed to see my husband flogged and called out to the constables to hit harder. Even if she's much younger than I, she might be thinking the same thing—about her father instead of her husband or brother. But if I were suddenly transported back home and walked round the dear old Marble Arch which as you know is where the Tyburn used to be, I'd pass nobody who would look at me and think anything like that because that kind of thing hasn't happened in living memory. But something very odd happens to us when we're cut off or think ourselves cut off from the place where things like that don't happen, but which is a place we still think of ourselves as belonging to. And the question is, do we belong? I mean any more? Do we belong anywhere? [14]

As with earlier instances, Scott suggests that what applies to one party in the Indo-British embrace applies to the other. In the first draft of *The Jewel in the Crown* this confusion of destinies results in an Indian expressing doubts about "who we really are." Here, Scott suggests how the separate identities of colonizer and colonized can become blurred and how all post-colonial countries face a dilemma in promoting their own identity (suggesting that identity and unity are defined through differences from others, through joint opposition more than through mutual recognition). In the *Quartet* he explores this for the British, but in the earliest draft of *The Jewel in the Crown* he also attempted to sketch its significance for Indians:

47

We are dangerous because, if we ever had it, we have long ago lost a sense of ourselves, and have been fair game, fair game for the moghuls, for the Portuguese, for the French, and now for 200 years for the British who are the gamiest people of all. . . . They have filled us with the desire to smell like them because we had no dreams of our own. We were not a nation. They have made us into a nation. They have created their own opposition. But it is not a nation of Indians that oppose them. It is a nation of blackskinned Englishmen, and no Englishman, black or white, will ever sit contented under a yoke. But when the yoke is thrown off we shall have nothing to oppose except what is left in ourselves of our Englishness. And when we throw that out, and we shall try to throw it out because throwing the English out has become a habit, we shall stop being a nation and start being fair game. In this way you see, history will repeat itself.[15]

The confusion of identity, which has its social roots in the idea of the nation, results in a feeling of permanent exile, as is found by each of the Westernized Indians, all of whom are as marginally defined as the Anglo-Indians: "In his father's India, the India his father *was*, Ahmed felt himself an exile; but an exile from where he didn't know" (S 474). For Hari Kumar, the process has worked the other way around (all he knows is where he feels exiled from), and his exile leads to a collapse of identity: "in India I could never become consciously English; only consciously Indian. Conscious of being something I had no idea how to be" (S 245).

Similarly, Scott makes the point in one of his lectures that British exile does not end with Independence (Perron also outlines how an English sense of superiority will persist after empire [D 106]), and in this he considers "fear" to be instrumental:

After all, the new race of exiles is there by invitation, commercial desirability, or need. They do not seek it, and do not seem to like it. As their forebears did, they long for home, but unlike them have no sense of grander duty to explain their exile. . . . They take with them into exile their insularity and their cynical jokes; their fear of being got at, of being used and then eased out. They are much the same as the old race of Turtons, but have no illusion of permanence to sustain them.

Their illusion is, perhaps, that they have no illusions. They look at India, and, ignoring the fact that we were directly responsible for it for a hundred years, find it revolting. The Americans call this kind of revulsion Cultural Shock. I call it fear. I know that it is easily caught and that the quickest remedy to mask the symptoms is prejudice, and the illusion of one's own superiority.[16]

What Scott calls "fear" in this passage, Rowan earlier called his lack of "self-confidence": in both cases the result is an over-compensation. The difference, Scott feels, is that in post-colonial India the British are too conscious of not "representing something," of refusing to identify themselves with their colonial history or to venerate those who were most directly affected by it; the result, an insular illusion of superiority, is the same (as seen in "An Evening at the Club" in *The Jewel in the Crown*). And exile is fundamental in the *Quartet* because it is the dominant social characteristic of the raj. It therefore forms the opinions, beliefs, and motives for action of all the ruling class in India.[17]

For Scott, the number of characters in the *Quartet* who consider themselves exiled is an indication of the marginality engendered by colonial service or subordination: a union of people cut off from the culture and society they represent abroad and a people barred from their centres of government and administration at home. The reality and misery of exile are brought home by its applicability to different situations: Teddie remembers exile in England (T 155), Ahmed feels exiled in his father's India (S 474), and Daphne in Srinagar (J 349).

It is Daphne who most realizes the illusion and the prejudice of the club mentality, of defining "circles" which comfort some but necessarily place others on the periphery or on the outside: "I'd built my own enclosed little circle, hadn't I? The one I'd feel safe in. A circle of safety in no-man's-land. Wherever we go, whatever we do, we seem to hedge ourselves about with this illusory protection" (J 434).[18] The illusory protection is composed of race, class, family, and also religion. These are all used to promote personal comfort and reassurance, but they are also used as weapons of political control because, as Kenneth Ballhatchet remarks, "the preservation of social distance seemed essential to the maintenance of structures of power and authority" (vii).

In this chapter, I have looked at the way Scott, often indirectly, uses themes of paradise, the Fall, and exile to parallel the history of the end of Anglo-India, and also at the way he presents the armour of its beliefs as inadequate for the raj. The crusading image of an imperial mission with God on its side, the ideal of a promised land, and of a just and benevolent paternal rule, are re-interpreted in the years of imperial eclipse as a parable of exile and a fall from grace, made worse by faded, decciving memories of one lost Edenic home and false hopes for the possibility of another about to be born. Scott saw this as essentially a British failure: "I think the promise was unfulfilled because the English never really identified with their colonies. . . . The administration always felt themselves in a sense in exile. I don't think you can successfully influence a country . . . if you feel constantly that you're abroad" (qtd. Weinbaum 1992, 213).

CHAPTER THREE

The Influence of Emerson

His current bedtime book was an Everyman edition of the essays of the American philosopher, Ralph Waldo Emerson. He had marked lightly but clearly . . . those passages of an essay on "History" which struck him as potentially fruitful targets for imaginative and intellectual inquiry, fruitful in the sense that they woke in him the feeling that he had spent his life thinking them and that it only needed a final intelligent heave of the rest of his acquiescent or recalcitrant physical presence to get the whole of him through the paper-hoop that separated hopeful belief from evidence of incontrovertible truth and spiritual actuality.[1]

Both Scott's presentation of history and the form of the *Quartet* are indebted to Emerson's first series of essays of 1841. Direct references are made to the pieces on history, self-reliance, and love, but general philosophical influences from Emerson's writing are evident in many more places in the tetralogy and help to explain the form of Scott's narratives. Most important is the essay on history, which takes a view here outlined by Edward Said with respect to influential eighteenth-century writers such as Vico and Rousseau:

underlying their work was the belief that mankind formed a marvellous, almost symphonic whole whose progress and formations, again as a whole, could be studied exclusively as a concerted and secular historical experience, not as an exemplification of the divine. Because "man" has made history, there was a special hermeneutical way of studying history.

(*Culture and Imperialism* 50-51)

The first mention of Emerson occurs in the third book when Barbie, by mistake, returns from the club subscription library with a copy of his essays for Mabel. Barbie has been struck by a line that appears near the beginning of the first page: "Man is explicable by nothing less than all his history" (T 67). The line has "caused her to catch her breath."

Soon she returns to the book: " 'If the whole of history is one man,' she read, 'it is all to be explained from individual experience. There is a relation between the hours of our life and the centuries of time' " (T 68). This is one method of design that Scott has used in the *Quartet*, where lives parallel both other lives and the histories of countries. Barbie herself apprehends this pattern early on: "She began to feel what she believed Emerson wanted her to feel: that in her own experience lay an explanation not only of history but of the lives of other living people, therefore an explanation of the things that had happened to Edwina and to Miss Manners of whom she had only the vaguest picture . . ." (T 68). Hence, the painting of "The Jewel in Her Crown" becomes for Barbie a representation not of Victoria, but Edwina, Mabel, Daphne, or Barbie herself, because its subject is the Indo-British relationship in which Victoria, who never visited India, was only ever the figurehead of a nation of exiles (T 69).

This is what Barbie takes from Emerson's first essay, and its construction and general philosophy of history are also used in the *Quartet*. However, before exploring that aspect of the tetralogy, it will be useful to consider the significance of two of Emerson's other essays that feature in the later novels.

"Self-reliance" is cited in *The Towers of Silence* by Barbie, and in *A Division of the Spoils* by Perron. The characters refer to the same two passages, and it is worth comparing their reactions since they illuminate the point from Emerson's "History" that the personal and the historical explain each other. Illustrating this, Barbie feels the personal meaning of the lines for herself and the people she knows, while Perron considers the lines in relation to wider historical and social forces. Both passages are read (slightly inaccurately) by Barbie — this is the first of them:

> "In the will work and acquire, and thou hast chained the wheel of Chance, and shall always drag her after thee. A political victory, a rise of rents, the recovering of your sick, or the return of your absent friend, or some other quite external event, raises your spirits, and you think good days are preparing for you. Do not believe it. It can never be so. Nothing can bring you peace but yourself. Nothing can bring you peace but the triumph of principles."
>
> (T 194)

The immediate effect on Barbie is to accentuate a personal crisis: she can no longer recall what her principles are. But, for Emerson, the personal and the historical are analogous, each dependent on its moral laws; in William Scheick's paraphrase, "The essence of the self, like that of the country, is reflected in the laws of its constitution" (92). Barbie will observe her principles, which are being replaced in the minds of her compatriots by other laws and beliefs, enacted in Britain's release of India — one of the last assertions of liberal humanism over imperial paternalism. So, for Perron and Rowan, the triumph of principles is an expression of the manner in which the raj hands over its administration to India:

"From what I've seen going on in the past few weeks I sometimes wonder whether the Political Department cares, so long as it can close itself down convinced that it's upheld the principles of the whole past relationship between the States and the Crown."

" 'Nothing can bring you peace but yourself,' " Perron quoted. " 'Nothing can bring you peace but the triumph of principles.' "

"What?"

"Emerson."

"Oh." Nigel smiled. "Did he say that? How apt. That sums up my department's attitude admirably."

"Not just your department's. I think it sums up the attitude of everybody who's concerned in what happens on August fifteen." (D 497-98)

Here, the triumph of principles is uneasily embodied in the eventual granting of Independence to India. Scott sees it as so late and so hurried that it is simply a last, tired gesture towards values and principles which have ceased to hold any meaning — the collective moral responsibility of one people to another.[2] Had Britain returned power to India after the First World War, then the history that contained Amritsar, national riots and protests, and horrific scenes of mass Hindu-Muslim slaughter would have been altered. Instead the British insistence on Independence on their own terms led to thirty years of repressive laws and growing hostility. The final "triumph of principles" is only a triumph of out-dated ideals, as Scott argues in one of his essays:

> This was a fact of History—1947 to be precise—but as Emerson said, All the Facts of History pre-exist in the mind as Laws. And by the time the facts occur, the laws— that is to say the moral laws—which create the historical events, are already old and tired, conscious of their own failings, their own built-in weaknesses and defects. (M 48)[3]

Thus, for Scott it was one of the last, sad victories of liberal principles to choose to free India, when the desire to assert those principles obscured the idea behind them — to bequeath a single country to a united people.

The other passage Barbie reads from Emerson's essay is this: "Society is a wave. The wave moves onward, but the water of which it is composed does not. The same particle does not rise from the valley to the ridge. Its unity is only phenomenal. The persons who make up a nation today, next year die, and their experience with them" (T 194). In Perron's reading of this extract, Barbie is one of those drowned by the movement of society. It engulfs her together with all those who share her "forgotten principles" and who are killed or broken in the course of the novels (including Miss Crane, Teddie, and Ahmed as well as the pair Perron names):

> Emerson was obviously too much of a peasant to appreciate the significance of you and me. Society is a wave. The wave moves onward. You and I move along with it. Emerson was writing for the Merricks and Purvises of the world. The ones who get drowned. Merrick hopes not to be. But he will be. Can't the fool see that nobody of the class he aspires to belong to has ever cared a damn' about the empire and that all that God-the-Father-God-the-*raj* was a lot of insular middle- and lower-class shit?   (D 208)

Perron, cynical and drunk, argues that Emerson, in considering the unity of society as merely phenomenal, is ignoring social politics as though unaware of "class rights and class privileges, of our permanence and of our capacity to trim, to insure against any major kind of upheaval affecting our interests" (D 208). Perron thinks class and property rights allow one to ride the wave, since he knows he can escape India by calling on his Aunt Charlotte (I will take this up again in the next chapter). For Perron, India, which used to be awash in English rhetoric of "moral leadership," has been devalued by its "owners" to the status of "property" for the well-being of which Britain accepts no real accountability: "A moral responsibility would be too trying. Even poor underprivileged Purvis was clearheaded enough to admit that. Property on the other hand can always be got rid of and new property acquired" (D 208). This is in fact a fault that Emerson notes in "Self-reliance":

> And so the reliance on Property, including the reliance on governments which protect it, is the want of self-reliance. Men have looked away from themselves and at things so long that they have come to esteem the religious, learned and civil institutions as guards of property.   (*Selected Writings* 152)

Barbie, who is associated with property (a picture, a shawl, her trunk, the Apostle spoons), lacks self-reliance, and this is in contrast to the two women who befriend her. Mabel and Sarah, Barbie realizes, have a resilience, an ability to endure. Rowan is immediately struck by this strength in Sarah: "Her quiet self-reliance had been the first of her qualities to impress and attract him" (D 147).

Sarah, like Perron, is aware of a moral responsibility that Britain has towards India. She does not rely on property in the way that Barbie relies on her trunk of missionary relics—an attachment which leads to her death. In contrast, Sarah has burnt her own past as a girl, and there is not one possession that comes to be associated with her in the novels. Sarah similarly does not believe in the possession of India and is self-reliant in a way that Scott shows both the raj and Barbie not to be, since each derives meaning from property and the past.

The second important essay of Emerson's is "Love." In *The Birds of Paradise*, Scott's novel about the quest for lost innocence and *agape*, the lack of love in the marriages of Bill, Dora, and Krishi is contrasted with Bill's search for fulfilment, for the birds of paradise, which he is not even sure can be found—though he has seen their dead bodies. He is given Melba, a parrot, as the closest imitation he will find. Krishi buys, and Dora gives, Conway the imitating bird, because it cries his name:

> Krishi said that he couldn't stand the thought of the parrot going through life shouting "William Conway!" unless she had William Conway close at hand to hear. Love's path never ran smoothly, he said, but there were limits to the obstacles that should be put in its way. And the parrot would be my personal bird of paradise.   (B 227)

But Conway, like Daphne, is separated from the one he loves, and the parrot, an appropriate simulacrum of a bird of paradise, constantly "mimics" Bill's longing, just as the elusive bird of paradise is itself a familiar metaphor for love. Virginia Woolf writes in *Orlando*:

> For Love . . . has two faces; one white, the other black; two bodies; one smooth, the other hairy. . . . Yet so strictly are they joined together that you cannot separate them. In this case, Orlando's love began her flight towards him with her white face turned, and her smooth and lovely body outwards. Nearer and nearer she came wafting before her airs of pure delight. All of a sudden . . . she wheeled about, turned the other way round; showed herself black, hairy, brutish; and it was Lust the vulture, not Love, the Bird of Paradise, that flopped foully and disgustingly upon his shoulders.
>
> (*Orlando* 108)

Similarly, love in Scott's novels always evinces this darker side. For example, the childhood triangle of William, Dora, and Krishi suffers its fall when jealousy erupts in Bill's petulant outburst of "I'm British and you're only a wog" (B 79). In the *Quartet* the animus returns in yet another meeting of a British man, a British woman, and an Indian man. Here a knot of forces ties Hari, Daphne, and Merrick, and, like Bill's resort to basic prejudices, Merrick's overt racism is recognized by Sarah as "our dark side, the arcane side" (S 398). A variation is also present in *The Corrida at San Felíu*, where the triangle of Edward, Myra, and the Godling is underscored by Thornhill's awareness of the jealous, destructive, dark side that lurks in all of us, like the *duende*.

In the *Quartet*, the relationship between India and Anglo-India is characterized by this kind of imperfect, Janus-faced love, which is also tainted by aggression, repression, violent outbursts, and mutual suspicion. *The Jewel in the Crown* opens with an image of "imperial embrace," the clinging that marks a love-hate relationship, and it ends with a similarly composed love letter:

> Such a marvellous opportunity *wasted*. I mean for us, by us. Indians feel it too, don't they? I mean, in spite of the proud chests and all the excitement of sitting down as free men at their own desks to work out a constitution. Won't that constitution be a sort of love-letter to the English—the kind an abandoned lover writes when the affair has ended in what passes at the time as civilised and dignified mutual recognition of incompatibility? In a world grown suddenly dull because the beloved, thank God, has gone, offering his killing and unpredictable and selfish affections elsewhere, you attempt to recapture, don't you, the moments of significant pleasure—which may not have been mutual at all, but anyway existed.   (J 447)

This common failure of the human intention to find love leads Weinbaum to argue that the *Quartet* "has no one human protagonist and obliges us to take as major protagonist the structurally unifying idea of love or union and to consider as human protagonists each of the major figures who embody this love" (1978, 109).

As with the earlier novels, the theme of love is shown on a personal level also, and it is here that Emerson's essay "Love" is mentioned. The first reference appears in isolation, introducing a sub-section of *The Towers of Silence*, though it has presumably been read by Barbie: "Romeo, if dead, should be cut up into little stars to make the heavens fine" (T 195; see Emerson 202). Its use as an epigraph encourages a wider reading than might otherwise be the case. There are two contexts in which this allusion is relevant for Scott: with respect to the fate of particular characters in the *Quartet* (Teddie, Hari, and Daphne) and with respect to any individual's power for goodness through love.

Firstly, it applies to Teddie Bingham, whose recent death is linked by Barbie to Juliet's wish for Romeo. Barbie thinks of Teddie as not approaching God's light, but scattered in a black universe of endless night. In one of her letters Barbie asks if Teddie's death has made the difference Juliet speaks of: "Go to the window when it is dark and look at the night sky and ask yourself this question: Are the heavens finer than they were? Teddie Bingham is dead, killed in action" (T 198). The answer has to be "no" because Teddie's death has not reconciled Anglo-Indians and Indians as Romeo's death helps to reconcile the Montagues and Capulets; and this is not least because there was no genuine love, even for Susan, in Teddie's life—or in the raj's. If Teddie's death has been pointless, and God meets Barbie's prayers with silence, then perhaps not only has Barbie forgotten her principles, as she thinks at first, but the universe itself is unprincipled. She indirectly wonders if the failure of the raj's love in India, represented by the absence of God's love in the universe, means it will be entirely scattered to the skies, like Teddie, in a tremendous explosion that will not make the heavens fine, but make them weep:

> I look at the night sky where Teddie is scattered and am awestruck at this kind of immensity. Unthinkable distances. Surely no prayer can cross them. . . . In all that terrifying blackness try to imagine no blackness, nothing, not even vacuum, but nothing. Nothing even as a thought. Space deprived of space in which to exist. Draw in the billions of light years of space and stars and darkness, compress and compress until all existence, all space, all void is the size of a speck of dust.
> And then blow it out.
> The mind cannot conceive of this situation. The mind demands that there be something and therefore something before something. Is the Universe an unprincipled design? Does God weep somewhere beyond it crying to its prisoners to free themselves and come to Him? If it is all explained by chemistry, that chemistry is majestic. It can only lead to the most magnificent explosion, to which God will harken while we burn and disintegrate and scatter into pieces. (T 198-99)

Without God's active presence in the world, there is only human love left, which, because it has its darker side, will lead to the magnificent explosion of Hiroshima that seems to burn Barbie to a shadow.[4] Shifting once more between personal and social scales, Scott suggests that it is also the neglect of love that leads to the partition of India on British terms: an assumption of racial superiority which equally prompts Daphne to insist that she and Hari go their separate ways from the Bibighar on her chosen terms of his silence and her lies.

The second area of importance for Emerson's essay in the *Quartet* stems from its argument that love is a power for goodness, akin to Romeo's tiny stars which make the world fall in love with night. Emerson believes that those who love on a personal level will also show and inspire affection and concern elsewhere:

> But this dream of love, though beautiful, is only one scene in our play. In the procession of the soul from within outward, it enlarges its circles ever, like the pebble thrown into a pond, or the light proceeding from an orb. . . . Thus even love, which is the deification of persons, must become more impersonal every day. Of this at first it gives no hint. Little think the youth and maiden who are glancing at each other across crowded rooms with eyes so full of

56

mutual intelligence, of the precious fruit long hereafter to proceed from this new, quite external stimulus.[5]

This is at the heart of Barbie's belief in the raj's ideals of "guide and correct" and in her missionary work—but now that belief is rapidly fading as she realizes that love is precisely what has been left out of both.[6] She tries to give Susan (and then the Rifles' Mess) the apostle spoons because they are "Twelve witnesses to love of the sublimest kind," and she has a similar attitude to the painting of "The Jewel in Her Crown": "It always seemed to me to be a picture about love rather than loyalty" (T 64).

A further reference to Emerson's essay is the inclusion of a quotation which Perron brings to mind just before he and Sarah make love. Scott here uses Emerson to state again his view of the ambivalence of human affections: "*The world rolls: the circumstances vary every hour. All the angels that inhabit this temple of the body appear at the windows, and all the gnomes and vices also. By all the virtues they are united. If there be virtue, all the vices are known as such; they confess and flee*" (D 333-34).

It is another affirmation of the force of love over the individual's *duende*. But in the *Quartet* personal love is always disabled. Sarah and Guy are the fourth significant couple to consummate their union in the pages of the *Quartet* (Sarah and Clark are never a "couple," and there is no hint of a love scene between Merrick and Susan). Each of the four pairs is different and each suggests a wider historical significance for itself. Hari and Daphne, lovers across an apartheid, are as doomed as Shakespeare's lovers. Their fate represents both the logical, brutal conclusion of the raj's "civilizing" mission in India and a continuation of the past frustrations of Indo-British fusion. By contrast, Teddie and Susan are the latest incarnation of the ruling British elite, driven not by love, but by his lust and her upbringing. The older generation, represented by Kevin Coley and Mildred, are shown to be loveless, and Barbie is appalled by the absence of tenderness in their "joyless coupling." Lastly, Sarah and Guy are the new couple who no longer believe in the raj but who find happiness together only very briefly and are effectively separated by Perron's need to escape Merrick—connecting them with Hari and Daphne. The similarity between the lovers, of a frustrated and temporary union, haunts Perron.[7] He links the circumstances of his and Sarah's love-making, perhaps also aware that it could have been Ahmed and Sarah, with those of Hari and Daphne's: he senses that the Moghul room is as redolent of the past as the Bibighar; that both couples' love-making has been a secret act, as though forbidden; and that their parting is hurried (and also insisted upon by Sarah, reminiscent of Daphne, who must hurry home). Consequently, Perron, a trick of the light making his hands seem brown, remembers the words from Rowan's report: "*We haven't seen each other since the night we visited the temple*" (D 337). As Allen Boyer observes, in the *Quartet* "every relationship between a man and a woman will be frustrated" (69), and so the personal love that Emerson hopes will bring out social sympathy and understanding is in fact repeatedly stifled and unable to bridge the gulf between people under the raj.

In the *Quartet*, the failure of personal love is both a synecdochic representation of the larger imperial failure and a symptom of it. Because of its inability to overcome divisions under the raj, love — spiritual, familial, universal, or sexual — is the most important emotion in the collapse of private and national attempts at alliance. Relationships developed under British rule, such as Nigel and Laura's or Kevin and Mildred's, are all unsatisfactory: Barbie's Christian love seems to her hollow, and the parental concern of *man-bap* a deceit; while Hari and Daphne's love is denied, Teddie and Susan's love is superficial, and Sarah and Guy's love must wait for Independence before, in *Staying On*, it is made public. Successful union, it seems, will not be possible until the imperial embrace is prised open and love need not be closeted in silence, in pavilion gardens, or in racial divisions.

It is Guy Perron, the academic historian, who is "the Emerson expert" (D 383), and it is also he who ends the *Quartet* by reading a translation of lines from Scott's invented Persian poet, Gaffur. Gaffur stands as Emerson's Indian equivalent in the novels, and the opening words to his poem at the end of the *Quartet*, "Everything has meaning for you," are a version of Emerson's pronouncements in "History" such as "Each new law and political movement has meaning for you" (108). Like Emerson, Gaffur sees all life, in the words of Scott's section title, as "Journeys into Uneasy Distances." Life drifts through an immensity of landscape and time, in which patterns repeat because time flows to "Places you can't see but which you also flow / Outward to" (D 598). Emerson, understanding history as "fluid" (117), expresses this belief in one of the above passages from "Self-Reliance" as "Society is a wave," because while time moves on the individuals that comprise the social wave change and usually do not realize that the form society is taking is the same as before. Gaffur's closing poem can be seen as a description of the events of the *Quartet* because the tetralogy can be viewed as another version of pre-existing laws, of the wave moulding new particles, new individuals, to an old shape. As a direct expression of this, Emerson sees all history as a cyclical process like nature: "Nature is an endless combination and repetition of a very few laws. She hums the old well-known air through innumerable variations" (114). Gaffur also makes sense of nature and history in this way. The poem says that the petal's fall and the change of seasons have meaning in the course of nature, and so do details in the individual's history. He cites "*The new clothes you wear at the end of Ramadan. A prince's trust*," and these are repetitions in the lives of court attendants like Gaffur and Bronowsky, originator and translator respectively of the poem Perron is reading.

Perron attempts to make sense of the past as a series of events that is finished but also as a history that impinges on and moulds the present. How the one affects the other is extremely important because there are several characters in the *Quartet* who have a false relationship with history, and they are either ruled by or indifferent to the past. Scott's use of the essay on history is the most notable in the *Quartet* because he is acutely conscious of creating a version of the past himself in the novels: a reconstruction which will also have an influence on how people perceive the present and act in the future. In contrast to Perron, another historian, Major Tippit, does not see the relevance of the past to the present or the future: "I'm a historian, really. The present does not interest me, the future even less. Only through art and contemplation of the past can man live with man" (S 28). Tippit seems representative of the historians who share the liberal instinct with Perron but who are also blind, like Purvis, to the lessons of the past for the present—blind to any "moral drift" of history into the future. This appears to epitomize an attitude discussed by Emerson: "The student is to read history actively and not passively. . . . I have no expectation that any man will read history aright who thinks that what was done in a remote age, by men whose names have resounded far, has any deeper sense than what he is doing to-day."[8] Tippit is unable to see the past in relation to the present and the future, to understand the relevance of the individual's life to history or vice versa. Malcolm Bradbury describes this inability to join the private life with the public world of events as a key problem for the modern individual, because each person

> tends to humanize history to the point of seeking his fulfilments within it. But he also tends to impersonalize it by seeing it as an unconditioned and independent force. . . . To put the problem in another way, it becomes increasingly hard to imagine, as Frank Kermode has said, the relation between the time of a life and the time of the world. (12-13)

In the *Quartet*, Scott tries to show how this correlation can still be imagined, and he hints at it in minor ways in the organization of the novels' details. Because large events are only the product of a generation's actions and principles, Scott charts a correspondence between personal and historic dates; for example, Mabel Layton dies on D-Day (T 386), and Barbie Batchelor, who retired "In September 1939, when the war had just begun" (T 3), dies on the day Hiroshima is bombed (T 391). But the relation is also there in parallels between Barbie's life and the history of the raj, so that in *The Towers of Silence*, the "past" is kept in her trunk as an embarrassing burden that few will bear any longer. Scott considers Kipling's vision of "The White Man's Burden" to have given way during the First World War to a moral responsibility to accede to Indian Independence. In the three decades that follow, Britain still fails to act, but fewer and fewer people believe in the "burden" of *guide and correct* principles: "The blame of those ye better, / The hate of those ye guard."[9] Those who still do believe commit the same kind of mistakes; Reid, for example, is shown to be of a Kiplingesque frame of mind by quoting him to his soldiers (J 277) before they confront the "rioters" with methods comparable to Dyer's in the 1919 Amritsar massacre.

Barbie's interpretation of the quoted analects she reads in her copy of Emerson confirms her personal understanding of what history means to her: her life is illustrative of history and the lives of others of which she has premonitions and apprehensions. For example, Edwina Crane's death begins for Barbie before she actually hears of it. It starts when Barbie is reading Emerson, and Edwina's picture of "The Jewel in Her Crown" is eclipsed or "goes out," while its glass protection—its "covering" or "graceful mask"—gleams:

> The light from the bedside lamp did not reach the farther walls but the glass that protected the picture gleamed faintly. Behind the glass there was nothing. The picture had gone out.
>
> She thought: I have gone out, Thou hast gone out, He she or it has gone out.
>
> She reached for Emerson who had not gone out but had been renewed and renewed to Mrs. Stewart's perplexity.
>
> "Each new law and political movement has meaning for you," Barbie read and was convinced that this might be so because Emerson told her. "Stand before each of its tablets and say, 'Here is one of my coverings. Under this fantastic, or odious, or graceful mask did my Proteus nature hide itself.' This remedies the defect of our too great nearness to ourselves." (T 84)

Barbie's propinquity to herself is about to be remedied by the distant person of Edwina Crane whose example shakes Barbie's faith and principles (Miss Crane's crisis is also seen as part of the larger movement of history: "the India she knew had died, so like a good widow she made a funeral pyre" [S 396]). Throughout the novels, both personal and public history, like Barbie's book of Emerson, are revivified again and again, and Barbie is touched by a contemporaneous act, the heat of which she can feel in her own life as she'll feel the heat of Hiroshima. She senses an intimation of Miss Crane's death that has meaning for her own:

> "The world exists for the education of each man. There is no age or state of society, or mode of action in history, to which there is not somewhat corresponding in his life. Everything tends in a most wonderful manner to abbreviate itself and yield its own virtue to him. He should see that he can live all history in his own person. He must sit at home with might and main, and not suffer himself to be bullied by kings or empires, but know that he is greater than all the geography and all the governments of the world. . . ."
> Suddenly she was aware of the intense stillness of Rose Cottage. Intense stillness and a faint odour as of something singed. She put Emerson away, got out of bed, put on her slippers and her long blue dressing-gown. She wondered whether Mabel had remembered to turn her fire off, whether something was in danger of scorching or bursting into flames. (T 84-85)

Of course, nothing near her is burning, as Barbie finds, but something is "in danger of scorching or bursting into flames." The source of this feeling, she will find out soon (T 86), is Miss Crane's act of self-destruction (the suicide theme is one which anticipates Britain's self-termination in India—and it is present even in one version of Merrick's death [D 571]). The danger she feels is actually there for Barbie's own life which will end synchronously with the "distant but terrible fire" of Hiroshima.

To aid her connection with history, Barbie has almost preternatural powers of conjecture. For example, she guesses that Sarah has visited Lady Manners (T 167), she fears correctly that she won't be able to find Mabel when they have to leave the mess (T 186), she imagines Edwina's words of "too late" (T 200), and she dreams of her own fall from the tonga. These border on ESP, and there is the suggestion that a heightened perception is precisely Emerson's apprehension of a relationship between our lives and that of others. Barbie learns this from his essay: "'If the whole of history is one man,' she read, 'it is all to be explained from individual experience. There is a relationship between the hours of our life and the centuries of time'" (T 68).

Beyond the relationships of personal history (such as that between Edwina and Barbie), and beyond the connections within collectively experienced history (Barbie as a synecdoche for the raj), all history is seen to have a correspondence in the individual's life. Scott refers to this insight as a "heightened perception of time and place and people and history—and of oneself revealed mysteriously in an extraordinary and compelling relationship to those things" (M 109). Perceiving this relation enables an identification of oneself with others and therefore a sympathy and understanding that Scott notes is lacking in views prompted by prejudice or "cultural shock." Scott therefore has Barbie read the gnomic lines from Emerson which argue that seeing our own lives reflected in those of others "remedies the defect of our too great nearness to ourselves" (T 84). The ensuing lines, which Barbie does not read, make the point in more detail: "This throws our actions into perspective: and as goats, crabs, scorpions, the balance and the water-pot, lose their meanness when hung as signs in the zodiack, so I can see my own vices without heat in the distant persons of Solomon, Alcibiades, and Cataline" ("History" 108). So Scott, like Emerson, argues that in history the individual's experience is mirrored, just as it has been said to be in the pattern of the stars, since both history and the zodiac have been made by humans. As noted at the start of this chapter, Said explains that "Because 'man' has made history, there [is] a special hermeneutical way of studying history." Yet, while history affects us and while people can learn from it, it must not be allowed to determine the individual any more than the stars do. An example of this point is Scott's story of the scorpion the Layton sisters see die in a circle of fire. Sarah Layton remembers the childhood event and sees a parallel with her own life which helps her to understand the exile's position, while her sister Susan, a scorpio by birth, has forgotten the incident but repeats the experience with her own child, endangering his life and loosening her own grip on reality. Sarah learns from history, whereas Susan is only affected by it; and this is emblematic of Susan's inherited role as true "daughter of the raj."

The source of the belief that all history is reflected in and reflects an individual's life is not mentioned in the *Quartet* until the last volume, although it is the first line of Emerson's essay: "There is one mind common to all individual men" (D 277). Scott explains this in one of his essays, arguing that he, like Barbie, like everyone, carries in his mind the luggage of "personal history and of the world's history." But, he stresses, though our contemplation of history can lead to a greater understanding of events, "One is not ruled by the past, one does not rule or re-order it, one simply *is* it, in the same way that one is as well the present and part of the future" (M 119).

His depiction of history as both relevant and recurrent works through-out the *Quartet*, emphasizing his agreement with Emerson that "All the Facts of History pre-exist in the mind as Laws" (M 48; cf. Emerson 107). That for Scott, the tensions, the race relations, the "Facts of History" explored in the novels, are relevant to the present is clear from his remark while writing the tetralogy that with regard to what he calls "the moral drift" of history, "the log at present damming up the stream is that of racial prejudice" (M 145). This helps to demonstrate why the raj is, for Scott, "the metaphor I have presently chosen to illustrate my view of life" (M 65). By analyzing this metaphor, and Emerson's influence on it, it is possible to locate the factors that shape history here, such as the relation of personal, social, and national histories to the present and the indifference of individuals to the past. It is clear that Scott has used ideas such as fate, "historical laws," cosmology, and karma to express the attempt of the human mind to detect a pattern in events.[10] In terms of Scott's use of Emerson's three essays, the moral drift of history is "dammed" by the opposites to both self-reliance and love: by the raj's prejudice and conceit, by its over-reliance on past values and by its blindness to historical responsibility.

Finally, the recurring idea of history as not linear but in some way cyclical or repetitive, regained a currency in Western thought with modernism, bringing exhortations like D. H. Lawrence's to "allow the mind to move in cycles, or to flit here and there over a cluster of images."[11] As a philosophy, it is most reminiscent of Vico's, where, like Emerson's, a mind common to all creates history: "That which did all this was mind, for men did it with intelligence; it was not fate, for they did it by choice; not chance, for the results of their acting so are perpetually the same."[12] Edward Said, in an essay on repetition, suggests why writers use this technique of charting connections between events in history and fiction, and in doing so he also provides a quotation from Vico that reminds one of Emerson and of Barbie's principles, of Scott's reconstruction of the past and the form of the *Quartet*:

> Finally, repetition restores the past to the scholar, illuminating his research by an inexhaustible constancy: "In the night of thick darkness enveloping the earliest antiquity, so remote from ourselves, there shines the eternal and never-failing light of a truth beyond all question: that the world of civil society has certainly been made by men, and that its principles are therefore to be found within the modifications of our own human mind."[13]

Vico's eighteenth-century Christian humanism also throws some light on Emerson's enigmatic pronouncements. Vico countered a movement to model the study of history on the natural sciences because history, unlike natural phenomena, is made by human beings. History is the product of the human mind and is as different from nature as a carving from a tree. Vico argued, against Descartes, that the individual is thus better able to know the truth of history than of nature: "we can understand human history not only because men made it but because our understanding comes from the truths which we hold in our mind rather than from certainties which we obtain as external observers."[14] Observations of history and of nature can provide certainties, but truth, which to Vico is a form of model in the mind structuring observations, is approached through the mind's interpretation and organization of those certainties. And the mind is better able to interpret that which it created.

Scott's concern with history, then, is twofold: he is interested in how it will be repeated in the future (because he believed, like Vico and Emerson, that it is always the same collective human mind that makes it), and in how people can learn from the examples of the past.[15] Emerson provides him with a way to address these concerns, the essay on history explaining "so much of what I [Scott] have come to feel, as an individual." With regard to its importance to his fiction, it explains "why the characters in my novels usually have—demonstrably—personal histories whose *weight* they feel along with the weight of their presents and their expectations for the future" (M 47). Scott found in Emerson a philosophy of history that he both felt and thought was true to his experience of the past. In the next chapter, I will examine the history he reconstructed on the foundations of this philosophy.

CHAPTER FOUR

Reconstructing History

Scott once described the British Empire as "that symbol of middle-class pretension and upper-class mercantile greed" (M 29). In 1945, with the creation of the Welfare State, an end to six years of war, and a new socialist government, this view was already sufficiently prevalent in Britain for it to tip the balance of economic factors weighting the future of the raj.

Then, with British domination of India at an end, it was possible to begin to assess it, and to attempt a summary of its political-historical significance. Using twenty years' worth of first-hand accounts and his own personal experience, Scott was able in the *Quartet* to survey and then construct cases for and against the raj with the concreteness of fiction over historical accounts: "History is always being re-written. Once done with a fiction is inviolable" (M 9). On the other hand, Scott's stories mix historical "fact" with fiction, and their backdrop of real events makes it possible to rework the history of the 1857 conflict, the Amritsar Massacre, and the Quit India campaign, behind the lives of certain affected people. A discussion of these influences will help to illustrate how Scott constructed his fiction by incorporating events that "might have happened" and that also convey the import of a more general history. The value of fiction over history is a common argument since Aristotle: "For the historian and the poet . . . differ in this, that while the former speaks of incidents that have come to be, the latter speaks of incidents that might come to be. On this account [the process of] making is both more philosophic and more worthy than history, for making speaks more of universals while history speaks more of particulars." Also, in metahistorical criticism since the 1970s, history has been perceived in terms of the tropes and stylistics of fiction. This view, which is reflected in Scott's novels, sees historiographical narratives as, in Hayden White's words, "verbal fictions, the contents of which are as much invented as found." [1]

Scott saw British India as a class-ridden society, a hybrid of official hierarchies and racial segregation, of caste systems and snobbery. In this light, it will be suggested later that class is used in a partial refutation of Emerson's view of the centrality of self-reliance. In the *Quartet*, class most commonly features as an example of prejudice and privilege, and of their vital influence on individuals and history. Also, Scott sees a close link between property and history, in the sense that both what is "possessed" and how it is treated explain much about a society: "The whole history of my missionary [i.e. Miss Crane] was suddenly revealed by her possession of these pictures [of Gandhi and 'The Jewel in Her Crown'], her history, and her attitudes, her good intentions, her liberal instincts, her failure emotionally to cross the bridge between East and West" (M 64).

But first, it is necessary to consider Scott's attitude to history and the primary historical perspectives of the *Quartet*. In the *Quartet*, Perron looks back on events and is able to adopt the detached historian's viewpoint together with that of someone who was involved in the incidents he reflects upon. He sees that characters like Merrick who disregard history are themselves disregarded by historians. Merrick is one of those "who lacked entirely that liberal instinct which is so dear to historians that they lay it out like a guideline through the unmapped forests of prejudice and self-interest as though the line, and not the forest, is our history" (D 301). As we've noted in discussing Emerson's essay, history reflects the mind that wrote it, but Scott refines Emerson's view by urging the reader to remember that Western historians, and therefore their histories, are for the most part liberal, favouring progress and reform. Illiberal figures receive a smaller part in written history than they play in the forces that shape events, not least because their principles differ from the principles of those who have most usually seen the value and importance of chronicling history. For Scott, the problems are that, on the one hand, written history elides some of the forces that shaped the past and so is a distorted reflection and, on the other, illiberal forces are left without a history, which means they appear rootless and spontaneous when they are actually new shoots of old prejudices. A liberal history of tolerance and progress is as likely, by omission, to foster pride and nationalism as its own values.

Scott believed this "forest of prejudice" to be based on ignorance and that through presenting the conflicts and mistakes of the past "his fiction would be able to reduce the weight of that ignorance and consequently of prejudice."[2] Some important figures become "unrecorded men," missed by the historians who look for the progress of liberalism along the path, but not for meetings such as that between Hari and Merrick, which "reveals the real animus, the one the historians won't recognise" (D 302).

Merrick's misrepresentation of past values in his persecution of Hari is a crime that only recorded history with its particular kind of selective memory will be able to forgive. One critic, believing that Scott is himself a victim of selective memory, deprecates the *Quartet* and other "Raj fictions which combine elements of realism with an inheritance of selective history, . . . of an imperialist heritage that warps creative freedom" (Couto 36). In fact, Scott perceived this problem and tried to circumvent it in his novels.

For example, Robin White (whom Scott admitted to using as a "mouthpiece for [his] own political and historical ideas" [M 66]) discusses history's selective memory, in terms of a sieve: "Only what is relevant to the attitude gets through. The rest gets thrown away" (J 333). White also refers to "unrecorded moments of history" and considers them to be inevitable, as the mind "simply won't take in the complex of emotions and ambitions and reactions that led, say, to any one of the single actions" (J 334). Scott acknowledges that the past is too massive for all its aspects to be documented in history and that any commentator will inevitably produce a partial history in which the selection of events will be conditioned by an attitude, whether it be Marxist, liberal, feminist, Tory, Catholic, or other. A common view expressed in the *Quartet* is that the liberal instinct has thus provided Britain with not just a liberal view of its imperialism but a history that stresses the presence of liberals before others (though this is a position Scott sympathises with despite its omission of "unrecorded men").[3] Scott implies that for the novelist there are two strategic defences of this position, despite its susceptibility to the above charge of selective history. First, one can depict malicious actions, rash or contentious decisions, and counter-productive forces in an effort, not to produce completeness or "truth," but to show some of the elements that are caught by the sieve of an adopted attitude. In the *Quartet* this is seen in a series of key dialogues that incorporate into the polyphony of the novels a spectrum of deeply-held beliefs about history and politics. Second, as underlined by his interest in Emerson, Scott shows how the novelist can dwell on the importance of conscience—which the narrator in conversation with Robin White calls the "moral drift of history"—and of the relationship between events, because he believes that "the present should always be seen in relation to the past and to the future" (M 47).[4] White explains why this is a possible way of breaking the limitations of an adopted attitude:

Perhaps, though, the mind can respond to a sense of a cumulative, impersonal justice? The kind of justice whose importance lies not only in the course apparently and overwhelmingly taken, but in its exposure of the dangers that still lie ahead, threatening to divert the drift once more?

(J 334)

Scott believes that the obstruction diverting the "moral drift" of the *Quartet*'s future, of post-Imperial Britain, is racism, and that unearthing its history in the *Quartet* reveals the roots of ignorance from which it grew.[5] Scott therefore uses prime examples of prejudice erupting in British-Indian history to embark on a fictional account of the imperial past.

Scott's foundation for constructing his novels was history itself, which he poured through the sieve of his own mental attitudes: "I studied the history of British India and attempted to pass that history through the selecting mechanism of my own experience and recollections" (M 123). As an indication of this, several of Scott's names have a historical significance which complements their use in the novels. The name Mirat is derived from Mirut, where according to some commentators the 1857 rebellion began, while Ranpur is based on Kanpur (Copley 60), one of the major sites of fighting. Most importantly there is the Bibighar, which is associated with one of the key events at Kanpur.[6] This incident, which will be discussed below, evoked a kind of British response equivalent to the Indian horror at the Amritsar Massacre, since "the atrocities of the Bibighar . . . were to inflame the attitude of the British more than any other episode during the Mutiny" (Trevelyan 316). The year 1857 also has significance as a starting-date for the explicit bifurcation of Indian and British sympathies and also histories:

> When in 1925 Edward Thompson published his powerful little tract, *The Other Side of the Medal*—an impassioned statement against British rule and for Indian Independence—he singled out the Mutiny as the great symbolic event by which the two sides, Indian and British, achieved their full and conscious opposition to each other. Thompson quite dramatically shows that the writing of Indian and British history diverged most emphatically on representations of the Mutiny. The Mutiny, in short, reinforced the difference between colonizer and colonized. (Said, Introduction to *Kim* 25)

Scott uses the two incidents, at the Bibighar and at Amritsar, as mirrors of each other's horror. Together they point to the necessary failure of the British hopes for a positive role in India: "The effect of Jallianwallah Bagh on the Indian mind was comparable to the British reaction on hearing of the Bibighar and Satichaura Ghat atrocities, though in the end more lasting. After Jallianwallah Bagh there could be no compromise, no trust" (Trevelyan 485). The Bibighar House was a shelter (like

Scott's Bibighar "built by an Englishman for his bibi or Indian mistress" [Trevelyan 468]) to which survivors of the Kanpur killings at Satichaura Ghat were taken, only to find their own deaths (British accounts of the "Mutiny" dwell on the Anglo-Indians who were killed, but the murders at the Bibighar were a consequence of an earlier brutal massacre of Indians):[7] "At the Bebee Ghur [or Bibighar] 206 women and children were imprisoned for thirteen days. News of the approach of General Havelock's relieving forces was to be their death warrant. One day before Havelock arrived they were all massacred" (Yalland 271).

This historical reference also has a wider significance for Scott. The grounds of the Bibighar contained a well into which the British corpses were thrown when the house at Kanpur was threatened:[8] a counterpart of the well at Amritsar into which Indian victims of the Jallianwallah Bagh massacre jumped to escape the bullets (which is again found in the image of the bones of the Parsees thrown into the centre of the towers of silence).[9] One civilian attached to Havelock's force described his impressions on arriving at the Bibighar:

> From this dreadful place we passed down the garden to the narrow well into which many of the bodies of the victims of the assassination were thrown. . . . When we got to the coping of the well, and looked over, we saw, at no great depth, a ghastly tangle of naked limbs.   (J. W. Sherer, qtd. Yalland 274)

Janet MacGregor's murder, at the house where Daphne Manners stays in *The Jewel in the Crown*, is Scott's equivalent for this episode of history, and in the first draft of the novel he included the image of "the old well into which Janet MacGregor was thrown, a bundle of bloody white flesh. . . ."[10] The picture of bodies falling, like Ahmed's body falling from the train in the closing murder of the *Quartet* (D 112-13), is a powerful one for Scott because the common physical movement symbolizes the sadly repetitive nature of human history. The fall is always that of victims of inter-racial conflict in Scott's historical litany and for this reason, as we've seen, Ahmed's body falls "out of a history that began with a girl stumbling on steps" (D 113), returning us to thoughts of brutality at the Bibighar.

His choice of political facts from Indian history under the raj is necessarily selective, as Scott is at pains to point out, but from the imprisonment of Congress members and the civil disturbances in August 1942 to the time of partition, Scott makes them prominent in the novels and uses them to frame the narrative. However, the novels also stretch into the fictional past in their histories of Miss Crane, Duleep Kumar, the Laytons and others, and into the future with the narrator's visit to India in the sixties. The narrator's interest in the Bibighar affair, which is kindled by reading Brigadier Reid's memoirs, illustrates how the *Quartet*'s future has become involved with its history. In *The Jewel in the Crown*, the narrator's observations register how attitudes have not changed significantly from the days of the raj inasmuch as Indian society is still shunned by the British despite official or legal changes; during the section "An Evening At the Club," for example, Mr. Srinivasan is blatantly snubbed by Mrs. Grigson and her friend (J 160-61). An assumption of superiority persists, as though in ignorance of or indifference to a history of violence and recrimination.

The parallel here is with similar attitudes concomitant with increased UK immigration in the 1950s, prompted by British demands for unskilled labour. Despite overall population decreases in the UK, bigotry and resentment culminated in calls for controls which were eventually introduced in 1962. Scott forges links between the 1940s and the 1960s by occasional comparisons, and by sounding echoes in the narrator's mind of the distant past, such as the connection between Parvati and the singer of classical music for whom the MacGregor House was built and who sang "the same song perhaps that the girl is singing now" (J 64). Scott is primarily concerned with history's relation to the present, because he argues that to understand a situation fully one must see it as a constellation of forces which has happened before and will happen again as the same human conflicts are enacted by different individuals. The past, both fictional and factual, foreshadows future events, and is not causal but predictive. This relationship therefore should be instrumental in any understanding of contemporary events, Scott feels, because the present can never be viewed in the way it is possible to view the past: "Here, on the ground, nothing is likely, everything possible. Only from the air can one trace what looks like a pattern, a design, an abortive, human intention" (J 191).[11] So, appropriately, Scott takes his central event from history and then records its repetition in the lives of his characters.

Apart from the Bibighar, the main building-block in Scott's reconstruction is the history surrounding General Dyer's order to fire on a crowd of Indians gathered at the Jallianwallah Bagh in Amritsar in 1919. The events known as the Bibighar Affair in the *Quartet* are in some ways a reconstruction of sides to this situation: from the attack on Miss Crane, the importance of Daphne's bicycle, the reaction of Pandit Baba, the charity of Mabel Layton, and the question over Brigadier Reid's competence, to the inevitability of contradictory and exclusive accounts of an event of great emotional and political importance. In other words, Scott explores a case of historical parallax where there is an apparent change in an event that in fact is caused by a change in the angle of observation (or, according to relativity theory, there is actually a different event because it is viewed from a different angle). Scott once wrote that " 'history seems to change as moral judgment varies.' For me this is what makes it continually alive."[12] This issue is touched upon in several of Emerson's essays, which note how one version of history can be adopted as correct: "Who cares what the fact was, when we have made a constellation of it to hang in heaven an immortal sign? London and Paris and New York must go the same way. 'What is history,' said Napoleon, 'but a fable agreed upon?'" ("History" 110).

The 1857 "Mutiny" is the source for many details in the *Quartet*. For example, the controversy over the feeding of beef to the Hindu prisoners (e.g. J 348) is a reworking of events that gave rise to the rebellion: "which people said started because the Indian sepoys believed they were to be forcibly converted, having first been polluted by the introduction of cartridges greased with pig fat" (T 5).[13] However, it is the "Amritsar incident" that is the principal ancestor of Scott's main story. In an earlier draft of the novels, Barbie explains what happened:

> Some men who were in jail were brought to the lane and beaten senseless with canes and everyone thought that they were the men who attacked [Miss Sherwood] because that's what that soldier said, General Dyer, but later it came out that there was no proof of that except in General Dyer's mind. I mean he was convinced they were the men, but officially they were beaten for infringing prison regulations. And afterwards when he'd given orders prohibiting public meetings and the Indians defied him and gathered in an enclosed place where there was only one exit he went there with his soldiers and just mowed them down without any warning.[14]

Dyer's brutality, together with the imprisonment of six Indian youths, was prompted by an assault on an English School Superintendent, Miss Sherwood, in riots following the Rowlatt Acts, which allowed imprisonment without trial and the continuation of wartime restrictions after 1918. This background provided Scott with the outline of the attacks on Miss Crane and Daphne Manners:

> "I am reminded," she said, "of Miss Sherwood. Amritsar, 1919. She was a school superintendent too. I never met her, she wasn't Bishop Barnard, but Edwina met her I'm almost certain. She had such a pretty Christian name. Marcella. Perhaps we missionaries are singled out because they see us as agents of the dark, although actually of light. She narrowly escaped with her

life. A Hindu woman rescued her, in that awful place, that little lane we sealed off afterwards and made people *crawl* down, on their bellies, in the dust and dirt, to punish them. I sometimes think none of that has been forgiven." (T 58)[15]

The parallels with events in the *Quartet* are manifold, from the first picture of Miss Crane standing at the end of a lane in the opening sentence of the *The Jewel in the Crown* to the repeated kindnesses of Indians to Anglo-Indians throughout the text.[16] With regard to Hari and Daphne at the Bibighar, there are also borrowings taken from the fact that Miss Sherwood was attacked while riding a bicycle, and although nobody was put on trial or found guilty of the assault, Dyer saw to it that "Six persons were whipped in the street where Miss Sherwood fell" (Draper 156-57).

The action of Dyer and the reaction of Anglo-India to the Amritsar incident, lauding the General for taking a firm hand at Jallianwallah, haunt Mabel's dreams over twenty years later in her misheard repetition of "Gillian Waller" (S 353). Unknowingly allowed entry to Mabel's feelings of guilt in the name she mutters in her sleep, Barbie connects this butchery of "unknown Indians" with all the Indian names she does not know or cannot remember. This is particularly the case with Daphne Manners's "Indian boyfriend": "Barbie did not even know his name. She began to have dreams about him, but in these dreams he was the Indian Edwina had tried to save" (T 72).

The bitterest allusions to Dyer in the story are made through Merrick, not only in his role as persecutor of six innocents but in the strength of his conviction, as noted by Bronowsky: "Dyer was another man who made a mistake, or acted controversially, and remained convinced to the end that he had been absolutely right" (D 156).[17] This partial identification is deepened by an aspect of Scott's view of history as "often made by ill people" (M 57). He is referring to the fact that Dyer was later diagnosed to be suffering from a brain disease which followed on from numerous other misfortunes: "although immensely strong physically, his life had been dogged by ill-health and injury. . . . With his violent temperament aggravated by physical pain, he was liable to overreact in an emergency" (Draper 24-25).[18] As mentioned in the previous chapter, Scott shows the behaviour of figures in authority to be always influenced by personal factors, from Merrick's social and sexual make-up, including sadism and his feelings of inferiority, to Brigadier Reid's concern for his dying wife and captured son. At one point, Reid considers his actions in the light of Dyer's (J 278), and the support given to his repression of crowds is comparable to that given to Dyer's: "Brigadier Reid [was] openly accused by the Indians of using excessive force in putting down the riots. . . . Nicky Paynton said, 'It seems to me Alec Reid did damned well'" (T 73). It is apt that Mabel Layton's guilty Anglo-Indian conscience lives on from the time of Amritsar to the time of Mayapore, and in doing so encompasses the final period of British rule: a rule which was at last acknowledged (though not by Churchill) to be no longer tenable after the 1942 imprisonments and the thousand deaths that followed the inauguration of the Quit India campaign. Pivoting on 1919, and spanning the time between the dates of the two most forceful challenges to the Empire, 1857 and 1942, Scott's historical allusions seek a connection between the crises of the raj which will exemplify the influences of race and recrimination. This connection he found most strongly at Amritsar, which was by no means a singular event, yet a notorious one that provided him with numerous starting-points for his key characters, particularly Merrick.

The personal influences on Merrick, Scott's most important incarnation of General Dyer, are deep-rooted and readily apparent. They are revealed by his description of Daphne as someone who "didn't give a damn who your parents were or what school you went to" (S 214). He might have added "or what colour your skin was," but this is the difference at which he repeatedly "draws the line." This need for discrimination is a trait of Turtonism noted by Forster, who contrasts it with his perception of Indian inclusiveness. In the *Quartet*, inclusiveness is significant because it is viewed as dangerous by Merrick but as liberating by Daphne and Sarah, both of whom Merrick chastizes. In his opinion of Daphne's lack of snobbery, Merrick reveals his own past: he sees the benefit in Daphne's liberalism, overlooking class barriers that have always balked him, but not in her distaste for barriers of race. He understands the prejudices that erect class barriers because he has been a victim of them, but he still believes in "line-drawing" to describe the moral dimensions that enable decision and action. In this he also resembles Dyer:

> [Dyer] was a soldier first and foremost with a tendency towards over-simplification. Life to him was made up of clearly defined blacks and whites; there were no subtle shades. . . . He sincerely believed that Indians did not understand self-government, neither did they want it. To them the raj was immaculate, just and strong; to them the British officer is a Sahib who will do them right and protect them from enemies of all kinds. (Draper 74-75)

Hari, from the other side of both the race barrier and the class divide, is an obvious target for Merrick, whose attitude is summed up in his sneer: "What price Chillingborough now?" (S 304). Considering the similarity of Scott's words, it would seem that Hari's fate in the Chillianwallah Bagh is a hybrid of Chillingborough and Jallianwallah, of class and race, of India and Britain (the name itself, Chillianwallah, comes from the site of one of the Sikh battles around the time of the "Mutiny"; it is mentioned in Kipling's *Kim* [101]). Sister Ludmila observes the start of Merrick's persecution of Hari as soon as the two meet: "already the Bibighar affair had gone too far. In those few seconds it had begun" (J 129). It is clear that Merrick's attitudes are largely explained by his personal history of social rejection, which leaves him an orphan and an exile, suspicious and resentful of others but also desperately needing to belong.

Salman Rushdie has objected to Scott's portrayal of Merrick,[19] but Rushdie in fact misses out the most important aspect of Merrick's character, which, I have tried to show, is history itself. Rushdie argues that the psychology behind Merrick's sadism is the cliché of a "closet homosexual" who is also, to steal another hackneyed metaphor from furniture, not out of the top drawer. However, his resemblance to Dyer, which is to say his historical significance as a representative figure, is more influential than his sexuality. Ironically, Rushdie makes a connection between Dyer and the Bibighar Affair in the *Quartet* but appears to think that Scott is unaware of it: "the calumny, to which the use of rape-plots lends credence, that frail English roses were in constant sexual danger from lust-crazed wogs (just such a fear lay behind General Dyer's Amritsar incident)."[20] Merrick's sexuality is also more complicated than Rushdie suggests and has its significance in erecting another barrier between Hari and Merrick (there is also a link with other covert sexual encounters from those of Hari and Daphne, Mildred and Coley, Lance-Corporal Pinker and an Indian boy, to Sarah and Guy, suggestive of the repression of sexuality under the straight-laced morality of the raj).[21] Sexuality is similar to the issue of class, since together they provide two further grounds for prejudice in addition to race, and yet class has a more obvious significance because it is the frequent basis of discrimination in Britain which is paralleled but superseded by race in India.[22] To Merrick this is of vital importance:

[Merrick] could be in a room with a senior English official and a senior Indian official and he could catch the eye of the English official who at home would never give him a second thought, and between them there'd be a flash of compulsive understanding that the Indian was inferior to both of them, as a man. (S 300)

The facets of Merrick's character are integrated into the historical concerns of the novels, and they are bound up with Scott's understanding of the imperial past. In this they contain elements of victimization and insecurity as well as superiority and prejudice, all of which lead Sarah to characterize Merrick's significance in the raj's history as "our dark side." While those with drive and ambition can prosper under it, the raj in the *Quartet* is still a society based on privilege and influence, not the principles which Barbie and Merrick (D 209) think still important. It is this that leads Perron to argue with Emerson's essay on "Self-reliance."

At times, many of Scott's chief characters reject Emerson's ideas. Barbie momentarily feels that history, rather than explaining herself, actually gets in the way of an explanation (D 208); Sarah finds the passages Barbie has underlined "tiresome and self-righteous" (D 222); and Perron challenges Emerson's view of "society as a wave." The reasons why he disagrees with Emerson are involved, but they constitute a good starting-point from which to examine Perron's attitude towards history.

To begin with there is the issue of class. In the statement cited at the start of this chapter, Scott characterizes the Empire in terms of pretension and property, and this adds a significance to an important distinction Perron makes between himself and Rowan from the upper-middle classes, and Leonard Purvis and Merrick from the lower-middle. As Emerson's supposedly ever-changing social wave moves onwards, Perron argues that the insular ruling classes who accept "not moral responsibility, [but] ownership responsibility" move with it, acquiring new property and assuming privilege which is passed from generation to generation (D 208). Emerson's essay on self-reliance calls for enduring principles, such as moral responsibility, and a rejection of those benefits brought to the individual by chance or "Fate," such as property. Perron, however, believes that most principles are simply a compound of pride and presumption, and he argues that influence can affect lives where self-reliance cannot. Thus Perron, illustrating his own theory, escapes Merrick by exercising privilege, by asking his aunt in England to use her influence.

His Aunt Charlotte comes to represent for Perron the indifference of the British to their Empire. Her refusal to accept any part of the responsibility for "the one-quarter million deaths in the Punjab and

75

elsewhere . . . confirmed my impression of her historical significance (and mine), of the overwhelming importance of the part that had been played in British-Indian affairs by the indifference and the ignorance of the English at home" (D 222). In a letter to his publisher, Scott emphasized that this was central to the entire *Quartet*:

> The overall argument of the sequence is that the greatest contribution to the tragi-comedy of Anglo-India was the total indifference to and ignorance of Indian affairs of the people at home, who finally decided to hand India back in as many pieces as was necessary so long as it was got rid of. Which is what happened. No one, that I know of, has yet said so.[23]

Aunt Charlotte thinks Britain should quit India, but only because all Britain's resources are needed to fund post-war rebuilding and the Welfare State. Leonard Purvis, however, though he shares Perron's aunt's view, cannot escape his misery in India and is nearly "drowned" as Emerson's wave of social change moves onward. What Purvis lacked may have been self-reliance, the subject of Emerson's essay, but, more importantly he lacked the influence of an Aunt Charlotte to bail him out after his "betrayal" by Westminster. Barbie, who also contemplates Emerson's notion of principles, will similarly, according to Perron's view, find herself without connections, friends, or influence. She is a victim of insufficient self-reliance only because she lacks the privileges of the upper-classes which cancel out the need to rely on oneself. Perron believes that Merrick will be drowned, too, because he is a victim of the "middle-class misconception of upper-class mores" (D 209): a man who has invented himself in the image of the superior exile, guiding and correcting "inferiors." For Perron, because colonialism is a masquerade of greed and property, this image was always without substance—hollow, like Conrad's Kurtz. For this reason, Bronowsky also considers Merrick to have (hollow) principles, to be "a man of the past" who believes in its real and imaginary virtues, whereas Perron, Bronowsky thinks, is "a man of the present" who sees the Kiplingesque guide-and-correct values of the past as a manifestation of a condescending sense of superiority (D 561).

Perron is an academic who has stayed in the minor ranks to be able to observe the people around him with detachment. Scott equips him both with cameras of the imagination (D 107) to record and focus his view of the historical situation and with an ability to tune his "inner ear" to the wavelength of current events (D 84). However, Perron feels too close in space and time to present-day India to apprehend its meanings. He finds "no connection between the India he was in and the India that was in his head," to the extent that India is "the last place to be if one wanted to retain a sense of historical proportion about it" (D 12).

Perron realizes that without a view from the future, "from the air," he is confronted by the difficulty shared by all those involved in a situation —"of the grand irrelevance of history to the things that people wanted for themselves" (D 84). Until the present merges into the past it appears misleadingly separate from its history, even for those who scrutinize it or those who insist on continuing to carry the past with them. And until the crucial forces of class and power are recognised, the differences in the movement of particles in Emerson's social wave cannot be seen.

The last crucial event of Indo-British history to be considered here will be the hasty event of Independence itself. Scott's position is clear:

> The only excuse for the partition of India was the promise it seemed to hold out of peace between Hindus and Muslims. Looking now—not only back upon the massacres of 1947—but [upon] . . . more recent pictures of riot and bloodshed, partition emerges even more clearly as the supreme failure of the British in wielding their power and exercising their influence.
>
> It established a precedent for the immediate division of spoils men threatened to quarrel over. But a land is not a box of loot (as Wavell knew). The contents do not by tradition have to go to the loudest-mouthed and the sharpest-elbowed. Unfortunately, once treated as if they did, the process of division is hard to arrest.[24]

In the *Quartet*, Barbie's trunk, which carries the burden of her past, appears as a Pandora's box out of which everything will fly except hope: for Scott its fate matches that of the Anglo-Indian relationship at Independence. The last recourse Barbie has to it is to retrieve the picture of "The Jewel in Her Crown" for Merrick. The representation of imperial heritage that Barbie has carried around with her for years is released along with the shawl and its imprisoned creatures: "She raised the Pandora-lid, stared and cried out. From rim to rim the trunk was filled with the creamy white butterfly lace" (T 381).

In *A Division of the Spoils* the release symbolized is many-sided. To begin with, it is not only that of the departing raj but also that of the princely states, which are the subject of an article in the *Ranpur Gazette* entitled "Pandora's Box." Scott has embraced this comparison between the raj and the princes in an earlier novel, where they are seen not as decorative lace butterflies stored in a trunk but as caged birds (this metaphor is also used by Sarah in the *Quartet* [D 363]):

> Well, then, Krishi said, the family joke was that the birds in the cage were thought to be like the British raj, creatures who took it for granted they

77

excited wonder and admiration wherever they went and had no idea that they were dead from the neck up and the neck down, weren't flying at all and were imprisoned in their own conceit anyway. Dora caught my eye. Krishi said that the family joke had misfired, though, because history had shown that it was the princes of India who were dead, in spite of all their finery and high-flown postures. The British had stuffed them and burnished their fine feathers, but as princes they were dead even if they weren't dead as men, and if not actually dead then anyway buried alive in a cage the British had never attempted really to open.   (B 217)

The elegant decay of the princes is presented as an Indian equivalent of the faded glory of the raj. The pact between them, their mutual dependence, their property surrounded by others' poverty, and their reliance on dead or dying traditions, all suggest how one would not survive without the other. Scott once wrote: "While the British ruled, the princes were kept going in all their feudal magnificence. Their fine feathers were kept shiny. But when the British went and all their lands were merged with the lands of the new dominion they appeared, you might say, in their true light—they had been dead all the time" (M 17-18). The maintenance of the autocracy of the princes was one peculiar fact of history, made not less but more unsavoury by what Scott saw as the betrayal at Independence when the British "left the feudal islands to their fate and right up to the last few weeks assured the rulers of those islands that no arrangement would be made with British India for independence without there being princely consultation" (M 19).

The last section of the *Quartet* is also entitled "Pandora's Box," and, in terms of the novels' allusions, Scott uses it to echo an opinion expressed by Lili Chatterjee in *The Jewel in the Crown*. For Lili, the meeting of a westernized Indian with the light and dark side of Anglo-Indians at the Bibighar Gardens contained the essence of an understanding of the last years of the raj; this event enfolded the historical significance of British India but also reverberated into the future, when the English "came to the end of themselves," as several Anglo-Indian characters in the novels describe the sensation of living through these twilight years. Daphne unlocked something, suggests Lili Chatterjee, "like Pandora who bashed off to the attic and prised the lid of the box open" (J 105).[25] This reference anticipates the carnage let loose by the impatiently departing raj at the close of Scott's five-year sequence. The British, having finally decided to leave, could not leave soon enough, and guiltily, even if some felt unavoidably, opened the lid of the sub-continent to let themselves and their unifying legal and administrative systems out, but also released the pressure of Hindu and Muslim tensions and fears:

the terrible reports of the breakdown of civil authorities in many areas of the Punjab, must make it seem that to achieve the objective of a political transformation scene in the long pantomime of the British-Indian Empire, the Viceroy, obeying the wishes of a well-meaning but ignorant British electorate, has found himself in the unenviable position of opening Pandora's Box and letting out all the evils that have afflicted this country probably since time began but which have been imprisoned, under a lid shut and locked by the single rule of British Power and British Law; evils which have not died of asphyxiation, but multiplied.   (D 525)

Partition was construed by many to be a continuation of the British policy of "divide" but without the intention to "rule," and in this way it appeared to exemplify Britain's past administration of India. The stratagem serves, for Scott, as another illustration of the British failure in India to accept a moral responsibility. The purblind continuance of a "policy" also typifies a way in which history seems tragically to echo its past mistakes. The solution was already familiar and despised in 1905 when Bengal presented the same problem to the British that India itself posed forty years later. Stanley Wolpert writes,

> Once again the machine, in its mindless manner, acted as though nothing were more important than bureaucratic efficiency, as if no human consideration—certainly no native consideration—counted. Bengal was, in fact, too populous a province (about 85 million) for any British lieutenant governor to rule efficiently, but the "cure" proposed by British India's Home Department proved far worse than the delay, confusion, and corruption that had long plagued not only Bengal, but every other provincial government as well. . . . The official scheme, undertaken without consulting or considering Indian opinion, was to create a new province of Eastern Bengal and Assam, in which there would be a Muslim majority of approximately six million. The remnant of West Bengal had a Hindu majority.   (273)

The partition of Bengal was the most significant event of Lord Curzon's years as Viceroy. It provoked a barrage of nationalist protest which was summed up by Gopal Krishna Gokhale's 1905 presidential address at the Twenty-first Congress:

> the whole country has been stirred to its deepest depths in sorrow and resentment, as had never been the case before. The scheme of partition, concocted in the dark and carried out in the face of the fiercest opposition that any Government measure has encountered during the last half-a-century, will always stand as a complete illustration of the worst features of the present system of bureaucratic rule—its utter contempt for public opinion, its arrogant pretensions to superior wisdom, its reckless disregard of the most cherished feelings of the people, the mockery of an appeal to its

sense of justice, its cool preference of Service interests to those of the governed.   (qtd. Wolpert 273)

Curzon himself had drawn attention to the earlier examples of the formation of the North-West Provinces in 1865 and the separation of Assam in 1874 in an attempt to justify his actions by historical precedent (Bhattacharjee 262). By 1947, partition has to be seen not as an isolated phenomenon, as a logical decision taken on the basis of consultation with Congress and the Muslim League, but as the last act of policy makers still embroiled in precedents for division.

Finally, like everything in the *Quartet*, Scott's narrator in the sixties is haunted by the past, and, while Lili thinks of Daphne opening the Pandora's box of the Bibighar, he thinks of her escape from the Gardens. Just as Daphne could feel the ghosts of the past in the MacGregor House and at the Bibighar, the narrator is told, "You keep on looking . . . down the drive, almost expecting to see someone who has run all the way in the darkness from the Bibighar" (J 105).

This chapter has aimed to show that this depiction of history as both relevant and recurring is in evidence throughout the *Quartet*, underlining both Scott's belief in a moral responsibility conferred by the past and his professed agreement with Emerson that "All the Facts of History pre-exist in the mind as Laws" (M 48). So, through "Pandora's Box," used as Scott's final section-title in the *Quartet*, the very first image of the girl running is linked with the events of five years later, when innumerable slaughtered bodies fall to the ground: the evils released by a history that begins for Scott with the Bibighar.[26] To survey this half-decade as itself a part of history, Scott places his narrator, like himself, twenty years on from the time of the Bibighar—when some sense of perspective can be gained and the significance of events gauged. Scott expresses it in this way in one of his most revealing essays, parts of which have already been quoted:

> India, to me, was the scene of a remarkable and far-reaching event. I see it as the place where the British came to the end of themselves as they were. It was, even more than England was, the scene of the victory of Liberal Humanism over dying paternal imperialism.
>
> This was a fact of History—1947 to be precise—but as Emerson said, All the Facts of History pre-exist in the mind as Laws. And by the time the facts occur, the laws—that is to say the moral laws—which create the historical events, are already old and tired, conscious of their own failings, their own built-in weaknesses and defects.
>
> The special fascination that India has for me is the almost tragic atmosphere I see as attaching to it then—and indeed still—as the mausoleum

containing the remains of the last two great senses of public duty we had as a people. I mean of course the sense of duty that was part and parcel of having an empire, and the sense of duty so many of us felt, that to get rid of it was the liberal human thing to do.

Getting rid of India involved the lives, then, of 400 million people. They say 2 million of them died by each other's hands. Returning to the scene in fiction isn't due to nostalgia, or to guilt. I return to it because to me the death and interment of liberal humanism is still a living issue. . . .

By Liberal Humanism I mean, broadly, the human consciousness of human dignity that began with the Renaissance and came to an end in the form that we knew it in the Second World War and its aftermath. Our imperialism was as much an expression of it as our reforming zeal. (M 48-49)

These sentiments are represented in the *Quartet* by the different but equally outdated ideologies behind John Layton's well-intentioned imperialism and the missionaries' reforming zeal. The death and interment of Mabel Layton, the Anglo-Indian who embodies the liberal human spirit in the India of 1919 after the massacre at Amritsar, is to Scott, as to Barbie with her spade, still an issue. Scott sees an awareness of the past, and its consequences, as a force which militates against the ignorance and prejudice that opened fire at Amritsar and which still fuelled arguments of racial superiority after Independence. Liberal humanism represented for Scott one set of the laws that Emerson argued pre-exist the facts of history. In his own language, he wished to chart in the *Quartet* a movement of human conscience and beliefs affecting a moral drift of events. As the narrator explains on the opening page of the *Quartet*, "There are the action, the people, and the place; all of which are interrelated but in their totality incommunicable in isolation from the moral continuum of human affairs" (J 1).

CHAPTER FIVE

Pandit Baba and Languages of Power

For its greater part, this chapter will deal with one comparatively short passage: Ahmed's visit to Professor Nair in *The Day of the Scorpion* (S 97-112). In this scene, Pandit Baba appears and speaks for the first and only time; throughout the rest of the *Quartet* his apparent absence from important events has a pointed significance for many of the other characters because of its uncanniness. The Pandit is an influential figure in the novels but more shadowy than even Lady Manners and less seen than talked about. Outside of the scene at Professor Nair's house he is represented entirely by hearsay and the views of others.

For the purposes of the subsequent discussion, it will be helpful to list all the pieces of information the reader gleans about the Pandit. By the conclusion of the *Quartet*, the following is known about him: the Pandit is believed by some to be one of the instigators of the Mayapore riots (D 407-08); his association with Hari Kumar is cited as partly responsible for Hari's imprisonment under the "Defence of India" rules (S 236-37); he apparently incites others to disrupt Susan and Teddie's wedding and thereby reveal Merrick's past (S 452); he is being investigated by the CID and is thought to have political affiliations with the anti-Congress Hindu Mahasabha and its activist group Swayam Sevak Sangh (D 317-18); he is a candidate for the identity of the "known" but anonymous INA connection in Mirat (S 467); he has been Merrick's persecutor throughout the narrative and is suspected of a direct involvement in Merrick's murder (D 548). As a teacher of language, he is professionally concerned with words and literature; the first mention of him occurs when Hari's Aunt Shalini employs him to instruct her nephew in Hindi (J 224). The Pandit's visit to Professor Nair is also ostensibly on account of language: he is working on a commentary on the *Bhagavad Gita*, and "[t]here are texts in the college library that Panditji wants to have a look at. . . . It is to inspect these texts Panditji is honouring us with a stay" (S 106).

Each of Scott's characters has an historical dimension (modelled on individuals like Dyer, Miss Sherwood, and Mother Teresa, or drawn from Scott's research into groups such as Congress, the INA, the ICS, and the "Club") which provides a viewpoint that can be put into dialogue with those of other characters who enter into the discussion of, to take the prime example, the Bibighar affair. The significances and interpretations of events such as the Bibighar are refracted again and again through new characters and ranged over by established ones, as evidence is sifted through their social, moral, religious, historical, and political perspectives. So, with Pandit Baba, Scott "ventriloquates" a particular discourse (that of Hindu nationalism, for example), infuses it into the Pandit's other uses of language, and places his voice in relation to other voices (some present in the scene itself, like Ahmed's or that of the official reports, but also some absent) which offer alternative explanations through words which carry other social overtones. At the most important level, these forces become instruments exerted on language to influence power, and they can work either to restrict or to expand meaning.

In his discussion of heteroglossia, Bakhtin argues that the most fundamental purpose of the novel is to put the variety of social voices into dialogue and therefore that the novel is inherently decentralizing and antagonistic to definitive meanings. This is in contrast with popular and often official discussion of "the" language, whether it be the national language, everyday language, or that defined by a dictionary:

> [Bakhtin] focuses on the opposition between the illusion that there is in society or literature a "single, unified language" and the reality that heteroglossia abounds in any society and that language itself is multiplanar and has a proclivity for "breaking down into separate discourses." Bakhtin distinguishes between the language of the novel and of what he calls the "official genres." In another one of his huge historical surveys, he maps the various points in history where persons or institutions, such as the church, have tried to impose a "single language of truth" or "correct language," despite language's natural variegation and flux. He charts an epic struggle over time between the forces of "centralization," which he also calls "the centripetal forces of sociolinguistic life," and the "centrifugal" forces of heteroglossia.
> (Clark and Holquist 269-70)

Languages are to this extent strong or weak, in general currency or neglected. The consequent imbalance of power becomes crucial to the way in which words are employed. The stronger the language (the more widely used, believed in, and unconsciously accepted) the less need it has to acknowledge or engage its competition, tending instead to offer the "word of God," the "official guide," or "the authorized version" in an attempt at monopolization. All other languages are thereby situated at the periphery and must either circumvent or challenge the centrality of the dominant language if they are to evade obscurity:

83

For Bakhtin, heteroglossia is not simply a range of sociolinguistic variation nor a kind of horizontal spread of dispersed speech forms: because languages are socially unequal, heteroglossia implies dialogic interaction in which the prestige languages try to extend their control and subordinated languages try to avoid, negotiate or subvert that control.   (Allon White 125)

Applied to the experience of India under the raj, Bakhtin's analysis of the connection between power and language reveals striking examples: from the basically imperialistic properties (through administration, legislation, and publication) of "Whitehall" or ICS language to the political connection between the English language and Britain's domination of India. Bakhtin contrasts the imperialistic conception of offering a "superior" language to a less "advanced" people, with the

Socratic notion of the dialogic nature of truth. . . . The dialogic means of seeking truth is counterposed to *official* monologism, which pretends to *possess a ready-made truth,* and it is also counterposed to the naive self-confidence of those people who think they know something, that is, who think that they possess certain truths. Truth is not born nor is it to be found inside the head of an individual person, it is born *between people* collectively searching for truth, in the process of their dialogic interaction.   (*PDP* 110)

This is the process of centrifugal and centripetal movements, of words as the sites of verbal struggle. The conflict between languages is uppermost in the Pandit's discussion with Ahmed where the issue is addressed directly because Scott again foregrounds the fact that an incident can be apprehended by those who were not there (to take the simplest case) only through accounts, in which words both represent the physical enactment of the incident and in a sense take the place of the incident itself. What happened in Mayapore in 1942 is described as a "riot" and also as the "spontaneous demonstrations of innocent and law-abiding people" (S 103). The authorities believe that law and justice were on their side and so what took place were "riots." The Pandit believes instead that "many people suffered the consequence of resisting unlawful acts by those supposed to be in lawful authority" (S 103) and therefore what took place were "demonstrations."

This is an example of linguistic relativity in which the incidents named are the same but their meaning alters with the language used to describe them (in other words, "what's in a name" is power: "riot" means that the authorities were in the right but "demonstrations" certainly does not). In this instance the two forces at work are both centripetal, attempting to restrict the meaning of events to their describer's political advantage.

In the scene at Professor Nair's, Scott demonstrates the ease with which complex issues are often reduced to simplistic descriptions in order to serve political ends. Ahmed is used as a sceptical mind through which the reader perceives Pandit Baba. Ahmed does not openly argue at any length with the Pandit but uses body language to suggest understanding and partial acquiescence without signalling his active agreement (S 103-04). What emerges as important here is the construction of "truth" through the use of vocabulary and semantics. To see how this is done, the following paragraphs will review the five occasions on which the Pandit argues his case.

At first, Pandit Baba instructs Ahmed, via twisted logic, in how to think of his father's incarceration in Premanagar Fort: "Do not think of it as prison . . ." (S 102). In an Orwellian doublethink that approaches a crude piece of deconstructionist analysis, the Pandit maintains that the jailer is as reliant on the prison as the prisoner and therefore equally restricted and confined: "It is those who call themselves jailers who are in prison, and perhaps all of us who are outside the walls. For what is outside in one sense is inside in another" (S 102). This first argument, as well as ignoring the relative power positions of jailers and prisoners, is destructive of distinctions and barriers (it is the Pandit's strongest inclination to a centrifugal approach) in an attempt to undermining the authority of the raj.[1] Baba then offers four arguments which become increasingly narrow and restrictive, as though after having wrestled "truth" free from the tight hold of the British authorities he now must pin it down again for the cause of Hindu nationalism.

He begins with the argument already mentioned: by invoking the English dictionary definition of a "riot" (S 103) he asserts his right to dispute its application to the Indian "protests" at Mayapore. This is followed by a further reprimand of Ahmed which accentuates the Pandit's *volte-face* from his argument over who is a "prisoner": "Loose speech leads to loose thinking" (S 104). To avoid this looseness, "It is necessary all the time to have the truth of things clearly in the mind . . . and to speak of them in truthful terms. . . . When you speak of riots you are speaking as the English speak. You must speak like an Indian" (S 104). The Pandit, with a sleight of hand, seizes the position of truthfulness in the name of "Indians" and insists on two mutually exclusive languages: "the truth of things" and how "the English speak." This is what Bakhtin understands as a centripetal pressure to reduce the number of possible viewpoints, to conflate a subjective view (nominally "Indian") with a universal one ("truthful terms"). In "Truth and Power," Foucault articulates succinctly the struggle that is being taken up here:

There is a battle "for truth," or at least "around truth"[;] ... by truth I do not mean "the ensemble of truths which are to be discovered and accepted," but rather "the ensemble of rules according to which the true and the false are separated and specific effects of power attached to the true," it being understood also that it's a matter not of a battle "on behalf" of the truth, but of a battle about the status of truth and the economic and political role it plays. (*Reader* 74)

The Pandit's supposedly strict, though false, appeal to logic and rigour is continued in his next and most interesting statement that "Truth is not divisible" (S 106). This deceptive statement lies at the centre of the *Quartet*'s explorations of history because Scott demonstrates that truth is dependent on the terms used to convey it—that it is relative ("born *between people*" as Bakhtin noted above), and that there are always at least two sides to any human event—any act of communication, any piece of interaction is dialogic. The Pandit points out that to say there is "some" truth in a generalization is in fact to mean that it is true in some particular cases and not in others. However, this substitution of individual cases for general ones is pervasive: it enables the Pandit to say "spontaneous demonstrations" and the authorities to say "riots" when in such circumstances it is likely that each is "true in some particular cases."

In terms of the Pandit's use of language as power, it can be said that having invalidated the British claim on truthfulness and staked it for himself, he now argues that it is also indivisible and therefore belongs wholly to him. For the Pandit (as for Reid, Merrick, Poulson and others) there is only *the* truth of the Mayapore "demonstrations," and it is his: this is totally at odds with the pressure of the *Quartet* to broaden meaning and perspective until the complexity of a situation is realized and one's biases are reduced by an awareness of the predicament of others. Within his own sphere of influence the Pandit's attempt at monopolizing truth is analogous to the official, centripetal forces in the wider social context; and, though I will explore later the effect this has on power, it is important to point out here, with regard to conflict, that Bakhtin makes a fundamental distinction between centripetal and centrifugal forces in his criticism, and this is of relevance both to the internal workings of a text, and to its position within the general cultural conversation. The centripetal he sees as the (unhealthy) tendency towards "ideological unification." Such a tendency is expressed in the way a culture and a language always works in the direction of the establishment of "sociopolitical and cultural centralization" (*DI* 271). This movement is in the direction of a closed system: the attempt to establish an officially recognized "unitary" or "monoglossic" language. . . .   (Messent 209)

The Pandit's language is only centrifugal when it needs to wrestle with the authorities' version of events—when conflict is inevitable. At other times, the pressure of his discourse is to restrict meaning for his own purposes of "ideological unification."

The final argument that Pandit Baba employs in his circumscription of truth and language is, interestingly, an official one. He states that Daphne's rape was "not legally established as having happened . . . , that in the end there was officially no rape and no punishment for rape" (S 107). Earlier the Pandit took an authoritative definition of the English word "riot" to back up his quarrel with the use of that term, and he now uses a similar method to remonstrate with the use of the word "rape," arguing that without a prosecution having taken place "there was officially no rape." This argument suggests, illogically, that since no guilty party has been prosecuted there can have been no crime "officially." It also implies that the Pandit recognizes official verdicts when they suit his purpose but not when they don't (as the official verdict of a suppression of "riots" does not). Scott is skilful in showing how the Pandit is strongly ideologically motivated and one of those individuals who Bakhtin says "think they possess certain truths" and so consciously resist or assist accounts solely on the basis of their political goals.

The Pandit's technique has been to loosen meaning where it serves his purpose to deny, but to tighten meaning where he is arguing for his own definitions and political ends. For Bakhtin, language is political, and its use reflects the user's perspective more than it reflects the object. The centripetal and centrifugal tendencies to restrict and expand meaning illustrate how language is a site of struggle and how Scott has reflected the historical and political forces at work in India before Independence, in the language of his characters.

The centripetal and centrifugal forces that are in operation in any conversation are most noticeable in the discourse of an individual, but they are centred on social standpoints taken by that person. While elements of the Pandit's political rhetoric can be isolated, it is important to remember the contextual significance of his utterances. Bakhtin argues that because each individual speaks in a specific place at a specific time, the audience of that speech (Ahmed, Professor Nair) will affect its content, form, and meaning: "Who speaks and under what conditions he speaks: this is what determines the word's actual meaning" (DI 401).[2]

By using this contextual approach, one can identify five broad levels on which Pandit Baba's discourse functions. First, as a teacher of language and literature he is professionally concerned with meaning and precision in the handling of words. An accuracy in the use of language is the pretext for most pronouncements he makes. This is an esoteric concern for the precise meaning of language which can be in the interests of truth but can be duplicitous, and is characterisic of an authoritarian, centripetal dogma. It is significant that the Pandit eschews the public acceptance of truths ("Only I can agree if you state simply that it was generally accepted through reports and rumour that there was rape . . ." [S 107]), while assuming or feigning impartiality and indifference to the parties concerned (Daphne, Hari, Merrick, the arrested Hindu youths). By contrast, throughout the *Quartet* Scott uses centrifugal techniques—such as multiple narrators—to undermine this centripetal pressure, which the Pandit, among many others, artfully combines with a supposed disinterestedness.

Secondly, if the Pandit is an "active" Hindu subversive addressing a Muslim who is also the son of a prominent Congress member, one would expect religious and political tensions. Conflicts arise early on in Ahmed's thoughts: "There was a certain kind of Hindu who inspired in Ahmed involuntary little twitches of distaste, the relics no doubt of the racial and religious animosity his own forbears had felt towards the forbears of men like Pandit Baba Sahib" (S 99). In this respect, the Pandit represents the role of Hindu defiance in contrast to what he would see as Ahmed's toadying to the British (and, in Mirat, to a Muslim ruler): "Do you not feel shame to speak always in the language of a foreign power, the language of your father's jailers?" (S 99). Ahmed's unspoken response is to consider the impracticality of adopting any other national language in India and to note that "it was fashionable among Hindus of Baba's kind to decry it, to declare that once the British had been got rid of their language must go with them; although what would be put in its place it was difficult to tell" (S 100).

As well as the division represented by the competition between languages in India, the Pandit tries to stir up division in Ahmed's mind by drawing attention to the fact that the generally pervasive political-religious divide (epitomised in MAK's political position and struggle for unity) in India is also present in Ahmed's own individual family:

"[Your mother's] family in the Punjab—they are perhaps more sympathetic to the policies of Mr. Jinnah and the Muslim League than to those of the Congress?"

"That is correct," Ahmed admitted.

"Since a long time, or since the political turncoating in the Punjab of Sir Sikander Hyat-Khan in 1937?"

"Perhaps, yes, since then." (S 105)

The third discourse that the Pandit cuts his teeth on is the political one behind his comparatively innocuous public persona of "teacher": that of Hindu militancy against English rule, of oppressed versus oppressor. Here, as we've seen, the Pandit speaks out against the widespread use of an official English language which mimics the power of Imperial authority. Pandit Baba insists that an Indian language is the "correct" one for an Indian to speak. Ahmed, commenting cynically on this discourse, also notes a pronounced difference between Indian and English uses of language, to the Pandit's disadvantage (Baba's rhetoric is obviously effective with many of his disciples however):

> In India nearly everybody spoke metaphorically except the English who spoke bluntly and could make their most transparent lies look honest as a consequence; whereas any truth contained in these metaphorical rigmaroles was so deviously presented that it looked devious itself. (S 102)

The Pandit's deviousness is integral to his subversive intention to undermine accepted ways of thinking. He officially denies that he has an active political role, yet evidently feels it is a charge that still needs an explicit, unprompted, disavowal ("I am not an agent provocateur" [S 105]) in front of a Congressman's son who is also close to the summit of power in Mirat.

Fourthly, there is the specific question of the Pandit's stance over individuals involved in the Bibighar Affair and his interest in MAK. Ahmed is sceptical about the Pandit's concern over his father's case, the Bibighar incident, and Ahmed's own position. The sincerity of Baba's rare displays of emotion appears to him forced and tactical:

> The Pandit's lips lifted at the corners. He was bestowing a smile of sympathy and of elderly approval of a young man's filial regard. Ahmed considered its quality; it struck him as no less dishonest than the expression of disapproval. How could Pandit Baba be moved to feel either approval or disapproval when the person who was the object of it was a complete stranger to him? Well, it is this that puts me off (Ahmed told himself), this ease with which people feel emotions, or pretend to feel them. (S 101)

With respect to his interest in events at Mayapore, the Pandit's political mission in Mirat appears to be to persecute and embarrass Merrick, for which purpose he has brought Hari's Aunt Shalini with him. He has no personal feeling for Hari, who "was not at all a good student. . . . Always he was attempting to forget that he was an Indian, . . . to him [his aunt] was a foreigner. All of us were foreigners to Hari Kumar" (S 108). The Pandit's interest in personal relationships is always conditioned by his political beliefs, and his view of a relationship like Hari's and Daphne's is cynical (and reminiscent of Merrick's attitude): "True intimacy is not possible. It is not even desirable . . . love cannot be felt truly except by like and like" (S 108-09).

Lastly, because Pandit Baba is concerned with both teaching Hindi and the nationalist struggle to rid India of the raj, he is aware of the political uses of language and the power of imperialism represented by the proliferation of English in India.[3] Consequently, he tells Ahmed not to speak in English: "You must speak like an Indian, and think like an Indian" (S 104). Here, the historical context is important and so are the individuals present—the Pandit's words are overtly partisan because Ahmed is seemingly accepting of Anglo-Indians (it is difficult to assess the weight of Professor Nair's presence because he is such a minor character, but his position of influence on the young would also require Pandit Baba to take a pedagogic stance on certain subjects). Ahmed should not speak English, because the English are the ruling power, a power which Pandit Baba opposes but to which Ahmed is largely indifferent. It is this aspect of language, its ability to denote power, that provides the most important context to the scene.

It is also an aspect highlighted throughout the *Quartet* in the person of one of its central characters who has two names and two identities. Harry Coomer was a privileged English public schoolboy, praised for his ability on the cricket field and accepted as a friend by the English upper-classes—though Harry had a curiosity value attaching to him as an Indian, it was an exotic one of royalty and romance, of princely states, wealth, and adventure. By contrast, Hari Kumar is perceived as a faceless, all but invisible Indian who claims he was brought up in England and so becomes categorized as a threat because he is capable of judging Westerners by Western standards (cf. Mrs. Turton in *A Passage to India*: "Her manner had grown more distant since she had discovered that some of the group was westernized, and might apply her own standards to her" [Forster 57]). Other members of the raj assume he is only "another lying Indian," someone they would place on a par with Eurasians who pass themselves off as "English" in order to gain respectability and status (e.g. Judith Anderson in Scott's early novel *The Alien Sky* [A 107]). Of course, Hari is as "English" as anyone in India, and yet this is not the key to success that his father was led to believe: "it took some time for the penny to drop that Hari's Englishness meant nothing in India, because he lived with his aunt in one of the houses in the Chillianwallah Bagh—which was on the wrong side of the river" (J 363). Hari's education is of little practical value to him; sometimes it is a hindrance, because of the surrounding context—he is an unimportant Indian in the eyes of the raj, so his excellent use of English is often seen as impudence.

The context of language is all-important because it is both an integral factor in the choice of words and determines their meaning. In England, when Colin Lindsey's father closed his eyes he couldn't tell Harry and Colin apart (J 220), but on the maidan in India Colin cannot even see Hari to talk to. Because the context has gone, the language they shared has disappeared. And while context conditions the language one speaks, it is also true that the idioms, conventions, and words used to denote, imply, and unite, can influence one's society. It is Scott's observation that when Hari left England he also lost contact with its familiar language and so became unable to communicate—as stranded from contact with his previous life of privilege as Philoctetes was, abandoned on Lemnos: "'Sister,' he said, 'what would you have done if you had received a letter from an old friend that showed you suddenly you were speaking different languages?'" (J 247).

Scott also explores the connection between power and language in terms of the way in which discourses necessarily exert an influence simply by addressing individuals. As Ahmed says,

> I shall destroy you, one man might say to another; and at once he would have a confederate, the man himself. Ideas seemed to have a life, a power of their own. Men became slaves to them. To challenge an idea as an alternative to accepting it was to be no less a slave to it. (S 102)

Physical hierarchies are more often challenged than ideological ones because they are more easily perceived. One individual can dominate another through strength or height, as Pandit Baba attempts to promote himself at Professor Nair's: "The Pandit—Ahmed now saw—was sitting on a double thickness of cushions. His was a commanding position" (S 100). But there is also a power in the utterance of ideas, a power which can "enslave," thinks Ahmed, and there is a hierarchy of discourse. At the hierarchy's peak is the use of the dominant language by those familiar with approved stresses in pronunciation and established forms of expression, vocabulary, and grammar. The dominant language can be defined as that into which others are most commonly translated: "Even Pandit Baba would fare badly if he went out into some of the

91

villages around Mirat and tried to understand what was said to him. He would need an interpreter, as most officials did. And the odds were the interpreter would interpret the local dialect in the language and idiom of the British" (S 100).

However, within this dominant language there are myriad other discourses which use differing vocabularies, signifiers, grammars, dialects, accents and intonations. Within the essentialist class-and-race distinctions of the raj the language and tones of the sahibs clearly connote the summit of power. Additionally, there are those who know the esoteric rules (which comprise what Bakhtin calls a "speech genre") of the most esteemed use of the dominant language but who are marked with the vowel sounds or expressions of a lower-class (e.g., Merrick's accent "betrays" him: "It was a good voice, but not public school. Aunt Fenny had already commented on that fact" [S 141]). Next, there are those, including highly educated Indians such as Ahmed, considered to be outside the "club" (to whom the language "belongs")—including Macaulay's "mimic men," educated to liaise between colonizer and colonized. After these come servants or those who know only a few commands and pleasantries from the dominant language, and those who are trained to recognize sounds and stresses. Lastly, there are those who, for myriad reasons of circumstance or calculation, are excluded from the dominant language altogether and who are therefore officially silent, politically irrelevant (this stratification is reminiscent of those invited or not invited to Turton's bridge party near the beginning of *A Passage to India*—the circles beyond circles of "humanity grading and drifting" [52]).

Within the system of exclusion, whether its calibrations are understood or not, language is a political battleground and words are weapons. Recognizing this, Pandit Baba militates against the hierarchy by choosing not to speak in English though he is able to: "His refusal so far to speak in English did not mean he spoke it badly or was not proud of understanding and being able to speak it" (S 99-100). Bakhtin comprehends this variety of speech as a model of the wider context of personal and public relations: "Language, then, is a register of social and historical diversity, of 'power relations and hierarchies' in any given culture" (Messent 206).

Any discursive hierarchy may of course run against the grain of other hierarchies (which is why the elite would place most Oxbridge-educated Indians below Merrick in the ranking outlined above), and this is what the Pandit, amongst others, notes in respect of Hari and Merrick:

92

But this was not Hari Kumar's way, who hated India, and wanted to be treated like an English boy, and spoke English and only English, and with what is called I understand Public School accent, and so was annoyed to be asked questions by District Superintendent who did not have such good education but expected to be treated all the time like a Sahib because of his white face. (S 111)

For sections of the the raj, the first rule is that the truth is white. Rao observes this in the case of Merrick's ascendancy over Hari: "Brigadier A. V. Reid unquestioningly accepts Merrick's version of the Bibighar affair, because Merrick is white and his version is the official version. A member of the raj system can do no wrong. To question Merrick's judgment would be to question English superiority, and go against prearranged emotional responses" (Rao 116). Merrick ostensibly justifies this view himself, in one of the *Quartet*'s many examples of dramatic irony, by asserting his immunity from "guilt" and the reasons for the raj's belief in his innocence: "I sometimes think that if I'd done something terribly wrong the rubber stamp would have endorsed it. That's its danger. It's a controlling force without the ability to judge. Once you're part of the rubber-stamp process yourself you could almost get away with murder" (S 213).

However, every social distinction by which an individual is classified — race, class, religion, gender, nationality—is conveyed through that person's language. The Pandit's own solecisms or "deficiencies" in English are recognizably "Indian." For example, he says "I do not know your father in person, only I am admiring him from the distance . . . and familiarizing myself to his photographs" (S 100). These dialectal expressions would be considered important "mistakes" by an inveterately class-conscious Anglo-Indian. Language is thus representative of the divisions which the Pandit believes separate one individual from another: "between men there are divisions and . . . there can only be tolerance, and absence of enmity—which is not at all the same thing as friendship. Perhaps the truth of this is most apparent to the Hindu who is born to understand and accept this concept of diversity" (S 109). Bakhtin, like Pandit Baba, situates these divisions within the struggles that take place in discourse, and he views language in terms of a contestation for the power of signification: in Bennett's paraphrase, "Language, far from being a neutral horizon of fixed and given meanings, becomes an 'arena of class struggle' as words are mobilized and fought for by different class-based philosophies" (80-81).

The Pandit, while at no point admitting that there is any real case to be fought, attempts to defeat the official language of the authorities in a way which Bakhtin describes explicitly in terms of dialogism:

> Any sly and ill-disposed polemicist knows very well which dialogizing backdrop he should bring to bear on the accurately quoted words of his opponent, in order to distort their sense. By manipulating the effects of context, it is very easy to emphasize the brute materiality of another's words, and to stimulate dialogic reactions associated with such "brute materiality"; thus, it is, for instance, very easy to make even the most serious utterance comical.
>
> (*DI* 340)

So, Pandit Baba takes an official word like "riots" and ridicules it by pretending not to understand what Ahmed is talking about and then by placing it in a context which denies it any credibility: "I remember spontaneous demonstrations of innocent and law-abiding people" (S 103). On the comic side, the reader is also privy to Ahmed's thoughts, which enter into the Pandit's dialogue and undercut his soberly expressed complaints.

To study this connection between discourse and power in more detail, I want to examine an individual word which contains an entire class-based philosophy within itself, *man-bap*, and place it in the linguistic contexts discussed above. To start, it is worth noting that *man-bap* underlies the novels because it is represented as the raj-ideal in the painting of "The Jewel in Her Crown": "an old picture of Queen Victoria receiving tribute, a very stylized thing, with the old lady sitting on a throne under clouds and angels, and Indians of all kinds gathering round her like children. *Man-bap*. I am your father and mother" (S 396). Next, it is clear that *man-bap* is part of a discourse summarized by Bakhtin as official or "authoritative," a type of language which perceives itself as monologic and so refuses to acknowledge that it is in competition with other discourses (one example of *man-bap*'s general success could be Hari's article on England and his old schooldays entitled *Alma Mater*, the traditional encomium meaning "bounteous mother"). Both Pandit Baba and the raj, with its ability to legislate and enforce through the law and the police, wish to monopolize the truth—about the civil disturbances, about the alleged rape—through the words that are used to describe them. However, for the reader, these words are necessarily put into dialogue with each other: "Everything means, is understood, as a part of a greater whole—there is a constant interaction between meanings, all of which have the potential of conditioning others."[4]

But is *man-bap* a part of authoritative discourse in the sense that it is imposed? It would seem not, because *man-bap* gains currency not through coercion but through the subtler, more common pressure that Louis Althusser (see 44-51) has called interpellation, in which "individuals come to 'live' a given set of ideological assumptions and beliefs, and to identify these with their own selves, by means of a process whereby they are persuaded that that which is presented *to* them actually represents their *own* inner identity or self" (Hawthorn 82). Though it might be expected that authoritative language would be enforced by military discipline, it is interesting how the members of a fighting community identify themselves with the paternalistic spirit of a foreign word which expresses an ideology of caring and self-sacrifice within an unwritten system of values. In the *Quartet*, Teddie recognises himself in this sentimental image of the "mother and father of his men" and loses his life for the kudos and the honour of the regiment.[5]

Man-bap is a discursive relationship fostered by the British-Indian military to reinforce the hypothesis of a family relationship in the army, thereby promoting authority and responsibility in the Anglo-Indian parent-figures and placing the Indian child-figures in a subject-position which requires of them, for their own good, their respect as well as obedience.[6] The relationship is to an extent legitimized by a familial environment of duty, protection, and understanding that extends to the families of the officers and of the soldiers. Its influence, though on the wane in the last days of the raj, touches several other figures in the *Quartet* such as Merrick, Miss Crane (T 269) and John Layton (D 345), each of whom is said to accept aspects of this discourse and uses its language. So, though *man-bap* is not a totalitarian language in the sense of being directly oppressive, it is powerful, often unquestioned, monologic in its self-belief, and more effective in purchasing loyalty and sacrifice than overt ideological strategies:

> Another pathology of language is "official discourse," at its purest a utopian language so compelling that no one would speak anything else. Official discourse in its most radical form resists communication: everyone is compelled to speak the same language. . . . Official languages, even those that are not totalitarian, are masks for ideologies of many different kinds, but they all privilege *oneness*; the more powerful the ideology, the more totalitarian (monologic) will be the claim of its language. . . . Speech falls away because— in the state such ideologies wish to underwrite—no mediation is necessary since everyone's thought is in step with everyone else's. There is no difference between individual and society.   (Holquist 1990, 52-53)

The individual's personality is subsumed in the group's collective identity, as though a conscripted soldier were not commanded but willing to make a sacrifice for others. Merrick says the following of Teddie:

> He went down there for the *regiment*. I told you there was a touch of old-fashioned gallantry in it. All that paternalist business really meant something to him. *Man-bap*. I am your father and your mother. It would have been great if he'd gone down there and called as he did and if they'd come out, hanging their heads, and surrendered to him, trusting in the code, the old code. That's what he wanted. I don't mean there was anything vain or self-seeking about it. He wasn't doing it for himself or for them. He did it for the regiment.   (S 393)

Such a monologic ideology is unable to accept anything outside itself, and this is behind much of Teddie's obvious stupidity and his inability to recognize the interested positions of others. For example, he assumes that Sarah believes in all that he himself accepts: "But Teddie would have made nothing of the Smalley image of Sarah. He surely never felt that she didn't take him seriously as a person; never felt that she took none of 'it' seriously ('it' meaning India, the British role in India, the thing the British were in India to do)" (T 97). *Man-bap* becomes both a conscious and an unconscious doctrine for Teddie—he knows he holds it, but does not recognize how it informs his opinions and assumptions, and he certainly does not question or reflect upon its political aims or implications.

In this way, Fanon has summarized colonialism's use of discourses such as *man-bap*:

> the total result looked for by colonial domination was indeed to convince the natives that colonialism came to lighten their darkness. The effect consciously sought by colonialism was to drive into the natives' heads the idea that if the settlers were to leave, they would at once fall back into barbarism, degradation and bestiality.
>
> On the unconscious plane, colonialism therefore did not seek to be considered by the native as a gentle, loving mother who protects her child from a hostile environment, but rather as a mother who unceasingly restrains her fundamentally perverse offspring from managing to commit suicide and from giving free rein to its evil instincts.   (Fanon 169-70)

Teddie's unconscious plane produces Merrick, who attempts to realize the actual situation between the raj and Indians. It is he who seems to represent for Scott the effect of giving rein to colonialism's "evil instincts," to the condescension and physical dominance that lurks beneath the purported benevolence of *man-bap*.

To reintroduce Pandit Baba into the discussion, it is obvious that his outlook and Teddie's are consistently divergent in all but their fixity, and the language they use demonstrates this—each has a privileged vocabulary which reveals his allegiances and conscious or unconscious beliefs about himself and the world. The two characters never meet, but a stone is effectively thrown from one of them into the face of the other, since it is probably Pandit Baba's discourse that persuades *someone* to turn the ideological battle into a physical one and cast the first stone at Merrick and Teddie, the twin profiles of *man-bap*, side by side in the Nawab's car. This event dramatizes the conflict between Teddie and the Pandit, two characters who never meet: which is one of the main aims of a thickly populated text like the *Quartet*—and the way it places their beliefs in competition has to be through language, through the characters' words in the text, which enter into dialogue in the mind of the reader:

> Bakhtin argues that language is where . . . struggles are enacted most comprehensively and at the same time most intimately and personally. It is in language, not in the nation-state, that social force finds its most realized expression: "Each word . . . is a little arena for the clash of and criss-crossing of differently oriented social accents. A word in the mouth of a particular individual is a product of the living interaction of social forces." In Turgenev's *Fathers and Sons* the Nihilists all go on about principles as do their parents. However, the young radicals pronounce the word *printsip*, whereas the older conservatives say *principe* "in the soft French way." Behind this small difference between consonants lie all the philosophical and political differences between a generation turning to German scienticism and a generation still espousing French deism. This difference between two possible ways of pronouncing a word brought into the open the major political and intellectual conflicts of the 1860s in Russia.   (Clark and Holquist 220)

Such a nuance in pronunciation can be extremely important and always confers a particular worth on the speaker and a specific meaning on what is being named. The importance and power of discourse is clear in scenes such as that analysed above between Pandit Baba and Ahmed, but also in the details of the text, demonstrating that language does not primarily communicate information but confers status: "Premanagar is most easily pronounced Premman'ugger. Old-style British used to call it Pre *mah*'n'gh, strongly accenting the second syllable and all but swallowing the third and fourth, which gave the Fort status of the kind enjoyed by a tent when it is called a marquee" (S 4).

CHAPTER SIX

"Kumar/Coomer": Divided Prisoners

> The present artificial unity of India dates back only to the British conquest
> and is maintained by the British bayonet, but termination of the British
> regime . . . will be the herald of the entire break-up with worse disaster than
> has ever taken place during the last one thousand years under Muslims.
> Surely this is not the legacy which Britain would bequeath to India after one
> hundred and fifty years of her rule, nor would Hindu and Muslim India risk
> such a catastrophe.   (Jinnah in 1940, qtd. Palling 97-98)

The contentious disagreements over the words appropriate to describe
clashes in Mayapore show that it is not only in the final volume of the
Quartet that Scott is concerned with division. His picture is always of a
fragmented raj, and Pandit Baba's quibbling is Scott's serious fictional
treatment of historical disputes: most particularly, the divergence of
opinion over the conflicts of 1857. Was the sepoy uprising a "mutiny" as
most English said, or the beginning of a "War of Independence" as many
Indians said?[1]

In Scott's tetralogy, the preponderance of exiles and prisoners, of
masters and servants, of pointedly juxtaposed accounts of events (from
"Civil and Military" onwards) indicates an interest in the division between those who in some sense "belong" and those who are seen as
"outsiders." For Scott, as for Forster and Orwell, the "club mentality" was
central to the British presence in India, from the crass assumptions of
racism to the political expediencies of divide and rule; and the search
for ways to transcend the schism is the hallmark of his sympathetic
characters in the *Quartet* from the politics of MAK to Sarah's breaking of
ranks (to see Lady Manners, to be a friend to Barbie, to want to know
Ahmed). In the notebook he kept for making general notes to himself
about the direction of the *Quartet*, Scott wrote that the main theme of
the *The Jewel in the Crown* was to be a British "failure." It became the
theme of the entire *Quartet*:

> Every aspect of this novel should be a variation on the general theme of our
> failure to unify. It should take into account the gradual fraction of the Liberal
> left on the idea that India *was* a unity, as well as the idea, happily seized upon
> by the reactionary right that it never was and never could be.[2]

In the previous chapter I mentioned the case of Harry/Hari, an individual given two names to represent the division of his world.[3] Hari's dual identity is suggested by his Indian name because Hari is the name of the divinity for Brahmins, the priestly caste who are "twice-born" (they are reborn at consecration) (O'Flaherty 144, 154). In this chapter, I want to consider how this split is delineated, challenged, and perpetuated, and it is necessary to begin by asking, as Merrick would put it, how the divisive line is drawn.

Hari's father accepts the belief that one may become "English" and that he can pay for Hari to be transformed into one of Macaulay's "brown Englishmen" (much in the manner that Shaw's Professor Higgins can metamorphose Eliza Doolittle into a "lady" and Dickens's Magwitch can make Pip a "gentleman"). This is because Duleep sees Englishness in terms of fair play, social graces and a code that comprises accent, attitude, and integrity. All this can be earned or bought for his son. That Duleep's belief proves to be unfounded in fact serves to destroy his image of Englishness, because the promise he finds unfulfilled, of equality to colonized peoples who accept English standards, principles, and behaviour, is itself one of the English putative ideals.

Scott was particularly interested in this because of what he found on his own trips to India in the sixties and seventies. An extract from an unpublished article entitled simply "India" demonstrates his anger at the continuation of blatant discrimination after Independence, when the two countries had been drawn into a Commonwealth of supposedly equal, autonomous nations:

> We drove back past the Breach Candy Swimming Club which certain zealous citizens had been picketing during the week in protest against its racial policy. The club's rules must have been drawn up long ago by a British Administrator, because nothing in them could actually be proved to show that a black or brown skinned body was unwelcome, let alone constitutionally prohibited. Nevertheless, of the people in the car, only I could get past the gate. . . .
>
> A carload of us went to Juhu, where there is a beach and an air-conditioned hotel. . . . In the old days when an Indian hadn't even a hope of reaching executive level the [beach] shacks were open to executives and above. Now with Indians even sitting on the board (in sufficient numbers to satisfy Anglo-Indian joint policy) some of the shacks here are open only to the Chairman and his friends. What's the definition of friend? An English acquaintance of my hostess once gave the answer away. "I'm off to the shack," she said, finishing a drink from Mrs. X's decanter. "What a pity you can't come."

We drove back to Bombay past different shacks. . . . Looking at [these] slum encampments I was bitterly ashamed. In my white skin I felt naked and responsible. Our parting gift to India after more than two hundred years of power and influence seemed to have been to leave her stranded in the twentieth century like a nineteenth-century whale.[4]

For the Kumars, the insubstantial promise of English paternalism is reflected by Duleep's personal history. Hari's father rejects his heritage, his family, and his country, to offer his son England; Duleep copies documents, faking the signatures of others, and in the same way he is suspected of trying to falsify Hari's identity; he commits suicide when the forgery fails and Hari is sent into exile to find the impossibility of his father's attempt to create a perfect imitation of an "Englishman."[5] The truth is reflected in Lindsey's father's appraisal of Duleep, an Indian who could neither "make it" in England as a straight businessman nor "make it" as a fraud (Lindsey senior remarks—unaware of its ironic application to Hari—"there's one aspect of the business that the bank says looks like a clear case of forgery" [J 218]). This is analogous to the manner in which a citizen of the Empire could be condemned for being Indian but also barred from being English—not only is Duleep legally an unsuccessful fraud, but his son necessarily comes to be considered by the English as a poor forgery also. In direct contrast to Duleep's belief, the elder Lindsey, when considering attitudes of superiority towards Indians under the raj, effectively concludes that the only thing worse than being an Indian is being a Westernized Indian: "The last man you could trust, these people said (and damn it all, they knew, because they had been there or were related to people who had been there) was the westernized Indian, because he was not really an Indian at all" (J 219). Yet, of course this is, crudely speaking, what the Empire offered to Indians: the prospect of self-rule after a period of induction and training in Western government. Duleep accepts this pledge and fashions Hari into Harry, an English boy. Harry is the Kiplingesque hero who has all the qualities supposedly contained in the epithet "white," except white skin.

When Harry finds that in India he is forced to return to the name of Hari, neither identity fits. He has to select a new self-image (ironically similar to Merrick's position as a "self-made" man), so he chooses that of Philoctetes, a forgotten, marooned castaway. The union of England and India has failed—the raj must go to an unfamiliar "home," and the old India is left fighting over its partitioned territories. It is only by rejecting his past selves, the well-heeled Indian in England and the down-on-his-luck English public schoolboy in India, that Philoctetes can go beyond the division in himself.

Scott develops his picture of India ruled by the raj along contrary lines of unity and demarcation. The unity is demonstrated by the common image of prisoners: both Indians and Anglo-Indians are encircled, enclosed, and imprisoned in the forces of history, prejudice, and the desire to belong.[6] The division is evinced in the following ways: first, the carefully described towns of the *Quartet* are split in two, separated into geometrically constructed cantonments and teeming baghs by the troubled waters that Scott uses as symbols of a common past (containing the idea of "the moral drift of history");[7] secondly, this violent past surrounding Indian and British union is mirrored in the histories of the gardens that grow beside the rivers; and lastly, in India, the Indians are "unknown" to the majority of the aloof and superior British who keep themselves apart—as though they were travellers to a deserted island. The theme of division, as suggested in chapter 2, is pointed up by the raj's exile from its compatriots: the "people we really are."

Both the unity and division motifs are collocated in Harry/Hari: "It was as though there were two men in the chair, the one you could see and the one you could hear. The one you could hear was undoubtedly Coomer and once you were aware that he was Coomer the unfavourable impression made by the shambling body and hollow-cheeked face began to fade" (D 291). His identity is a hybrid of Indians and English, yet he is at home with neither under the raj and becomes an outcast. For Scott, the rejection and loss of the identity of "Kumar/Coomer" (D 292) is the failure of the raj.

One aspect of the emphasis on division is the use Scott makes of the partitioning of Indian cities and towns. *The Day of the Scorpion* begins with a prologue set in the 1960s which describes a Muslim woman visiting, the writer imagines, the Great Mosque at the heart of the predominantly Hindu town of Ranpur. The writer looks for signs of the past British occupation, "these island people" (S 3), and, while finding many functional and purposeful buildings, he is most impressed by "something for which there is no memorial but which all these things collectively bear witness to: the fact that here in Ranpur, and in places like Ranpur, the British came to the end of themselves as they were" (S 3). This simple picture, of a Muslim hurrying through a Hindu city stamped with the personality of the British, introduces many themes—of expiry, of difference and division, of "island people"—which *The Day of the Scorpion* builds upon images from *The Jewel in the Crown*. Ranpur, like Mayapore, and like Mirat, which is encountered later in the novel, is a divided town.

101

The split shows itself in its layout as well as its inhabitants. The towns are all bisected by water: the water which Scott uses to reflect the racially-based separation of East from West and into which Sister Ludmila believes Daphne Manners threw herself—a plunge Daphne herself realized was dangerous "because that is the last division of all, isn't it? The colour of the skin" (J 448).

Mayapore is sliced in two by its river, which is crossed by the Bibighar and Mandir Gate bridges.[8] Similarly, "there were two Mirats . . . separated by an expanse of water" (S 130), and in Ranpur there is the "sacred" river where "bridges connect the north to the south bank" (S 2). Scott's repeated depiction of the two sides of Ranpur joined by the river, which few will enter though many pass over, is of space to "the north where lateral and tangential industrial development has broken the landscape with chimneys taller than any minaret," and to the south, "a warren of narrow streets and chowks in which . . . the confusion seems to be almost deliberate, the result of recognition of a need to huddle together in order not to be destroyed" (S 2). Scott's descriptions highlight the difference between the closeness of the Indian community, teeming with life, and the comparatively alien geometry of the British invaders who wanted above all to recreate a piece of "home."[9] The division between Indian and Anglo-Indian communities is pointed up in the *Quartet* by the descriptive stress on the policy of apartheid present in each town.

The Day of the Scorpion opens with two images (S 6): the town of Ranpur and the fort at Premanagar. The first I have touched on, but this second image places another construction on the novel's presentation of the people and their towns. As noted above, the prologue begins with a Muslim woman. She is hidden except for her eyes which peer out from the slit in her burkha. She is walking through a predominantly Hindu town and closed in by relics of former British power. It is an image analogous to the picture of the politician Kasim looking out through the bars of his prison: a Muslim member of the predominantly Hindu Congress constrained by the British in the decayed stronghold of the fort at Premanagar (the Muslim Nawab of a largely Hindu Mirat is in a similar position). These are the first two prisoners, but as the *Quartet* continues, more and more of the characters are entrapped by clothing, walls, fire, or ideology. Scott suggests that this common fate, of exile, isolation, and entrapment unites characters otherwise divided by empire, religion, race, or politics.

The first book of *The Day of the Scorpion*, called "The Prisoners in the Fort,"[10] establishes fully the fort as an emblem of all the unfamiliar

102

surroundings that enclose characters. It is one of the most far-reaching and powerful images in the novels, and widens out to include all Scott's characters, no matter whether they be official "prisoners," like Kasim, or their guards, like Major Tippit—both are held inside the fort. This image of the raj imprisoning both Indians and Anglo-Indians begins with the Laytons "holding a fort together" (S 318) and persists to the last novel where even little Edward Bingham is found by Perron "guarding the fort while Ronald is away" (D 503). Scott, in fact, is asking us to sympathize with Pandit Baba's exceptionable argument, scrutinized in the last chapter, that the jailer is as reliant on the prison as the prisoner: "It is those who call themselves jailers who are in prison, and perhaps all of us who are outside the walls. For what is outside in one sense is inside in another" (S 102). Scott reforms this view by showing that the Anglo-Indian jailers, like Tippit at Premanagar but also the Laytons, are also inside their prison.[11]

Scott unites some of the prisoners through his process of reverse exploration, of investigating the back of the image. Any reader coming to *The Day of the Scorpion* from *The Jewel in the Crown* will be prompted by the title "The Prisoners in the Fort" to think of Hari Kumar, and the other Hindu youths, detained by Merrick on mere suspicion of sedition under the Defence of India laws. Yet Hari will not be introduced until the second book, "Orders of Release," by which time the reader will be expecting this title to refer to Kasim. In this way, Scott coaxes the reader into making connections by implying one character or place through a suggestive phrase but developing an entirely different part of the narrative.

The prisoners Scott suggests most often are the British rulers, forced to guard an Indian prison of their own making or imprisoned while defending the raj's claim to that country—like Colonel Layton and Alec Reid's son—in Germany, Malaya, or Japan.[12] There is however a double-aspect in the people and images of Scott's raj that needs to be explained (e.g., two aspects are expressed through these pairs: Susan and Sarah, butterflies and fireflies, geometry and patternlessness, warmth and burning, inclusion and exclusion): a duality which does not necessarily, as in the theological duality of good and evil, posit opposed qualities but ones which nonetheless, as in the philosophical duality of mind and matter, co-exist like the characteristics of the Muirs and Laytons inherited by Sarah and Susan.

Book one of *The Day of the Scorpion* concludes with Sarah Layton finding one type of comfort in enclosure: "she entered the geometrical pattern of light and the circle of safety" (S 220, repeated D 132). This is a description of the reassurance afforded by the Western halves of the towns considered above. However, in similar terms Scott provides a very dissimilar circle of danger for the Laytons: "when Susan Mem set fire to the kerosene and the flames leapt, arcing their way round in a geometrical perfection, Minnie . . . entered the circle and picked the child up and carried it to safety" (S 483). Such two-sided imagery is common in the novels and warns the reader from ascribing a meaning too readily to passages in isolation from the *Quartet*'s overall pattern.

Scott's ambivalence stems from his view of positive and negative qualities inherent in any enterprise. As will be shown below, he confronts the paradoxical effects of his chosen images: light covers darkness but can also reveal ugliness, heat warms but can also burn, buildings shelter but can also imprison, and the mesh of a mosquito net protects but can also entangle.

The theme of containment is most potently expressed in a variation on this last example. Scott's chief image for the representatives of the raj is a christening shawl whose pattern imprisons numerous delicately stitched lace butterflies. The narrator anticipates this in *The Jewel in the Crown* when he describes his naive "lepidopteristic intention to pin down the truth about Miss Crane, Miss Manners, and young Kumar" (J 88). Imprisoned, entangled butterflies is one description of the Laytons: John Layton, locked in a prison camp; Susan Layton, unable to bear very much reality and immured behind bars for her own good; and Sarah Layton, "the tough little butterfly of Aunt Fenny's affectionate imagination" (S 411), so different from Susan, but also locked in: "[Sarah] grasped the key. It weighed nothing. What it would open was a prison of a kind. . . . Through the net she saw blurred pictures of a stranger dressing" (S 439). While nets keep out unwanted insects, they can also entangle those beneath them, as a pupal Perron finds two novels later: "That night, fearful of snakes, of ghosts, he cocooned himself in a sheet, within the security of his mosquito-net shrouded bed. . . . He woke while it was still dark, from a nightmare that had transformed him into a huge butterfly that beat and beat and fragmented its wings against the imprisoning mesh of the net" (D 550-51). These recurring images of nets and prisoners are reminiscent of Plato's poetic myths explaining the human condition. The British are repeatedly shown by Scott as caught, trapped, veiled, or netted, and the vision that they have of their mission in India is like the Platonic ideal beyond the cave of shadows—something out of reach but for which a few people strive or stretch their imagination. The ideal, uncontaminated by human flesh and failing, undying and resplendent, is only glimpsed on

104

earth in the ephemeral beauty of such frail insects as free butterflies, just as Sarah stands "amazed at . . . the antics of a pair of butterflies whom Teddie's death had not affected" (S 315). As a comment on the illusion of British India, Scott paints a picture of misguided and purblind prisoners, mistaking their charades for reality (he chose the name Mayapore because *Maya* means illusion).

In Plato's cave the only things that can be seen are shadows thrown onto a wall by a nearby fire.[13] One critic describes the inhabitants thus:

> Within the cave are prisoners, chained so that they cannot turn and see the entrance: on the wall at the back of the cave are thrown the shadows of those who pass behind the prisoners, and these passing shadows are all that they can perceive. If they were unchained and turned to face the entrance of the cave they would be dazzled. Human beings are like the prisoners: they think that the world which they behold is the reality.   (Watson 304)

In the middle of the twentieth century, the members of the raj think their lives are real, but to Scott they perceive and preserve a false, anachronistic imitation of the supremely influential people they used to be.[14] This is so different from "the people they really are" in a Britain of economic decline and socialist sympathy aiming towards a welfare state. Anglo-Indians exist in a twilight world, and the flash of Hiroshima, of post-war scepticism over any form of totalitarianism, and of anti-imperialist egalitarianism, will scorch and blind Scott's cave-dwellers, used to the illusion of sahibs and servants. This is partly why Kasim, in his letter at the end of *The Towers of Silence*, wonders which of the two events, a Labour election victory or the Hiroshima bombing, will be the more determinate of India's future. Together, he supposes, they will mean that British opinion will be against further conflict and therefore in favour of Independence. Meanwhile, Scott's prisoners are hidden away like scorpions, who cannot bear heat and fire but hide "in holes and crevices of the crumbling stone" (S 398).

As noted above, characters react differently to their incarceration. For example, the dissimilarities of Sarah and Susan are revealed in their different experiences of the heat of India.[15] They, like all Anglo-Indians in the novel, but especially those who are surrounded by fire (Miss Crane, Teddie, baby Edward, and Barbie) are seen as akin to the scorpion: "no longer sheltered by the carapace of our history which is leaving us behind. And one day we shall lie exposed, in our tender skins" (S 398). Sarah, however, who is able to reflect on this point, is less tender than most. She has "a certain set to her bones, a toughness to her skin" (S 82). This is attributed to her inheritance, from the side of her family

105

that has had to strengthen its self-belief against climates and criticisms: "authentic bony Layton . . . There was a toughness in the Layton face that weathered storms" (S 142). She has adopted the same ability to repress disabling thoughts and emotions that Barbie senses in Mabel Layton: "She puts her hand on my arm and I am *imprisoned* by her capacity to survive" (T 199, my emphasis). Susan, however, is tender-skinned and has inherited less of the Layton and more of the Muir characteristics (and those of her real grandmother who "hadn't been quite up to meeting the demands the country made on white people" [S 58]). She is, consequently, her mother's child. Mildred, though strong, drinks to numb her feelings, to shield her from responsibility and criticism, while Susan looks for security under the protection of husbands who embody past values: Teddie Bingham, who is scorched to death because of his belief in the outdated concept of *man-bap*, and Ronald Merrick, who is another kind of "anachronism" (S 194)—a fact that even Susan realizes in her unconscious associations: "When Aunt Fenny told me last week that Ronnie was dead I thought first of a snake. Or of a scorpion. I've always been terrified of scorpions" (D 512).[16] As children Susan and Sarah were protected from these "insects" by "Dost Mohammed the head *mali* who knew the ways of snakes and scorpions so well that neither child ever saw a live snake and only one living scorpion" (S 67). What Mabel Layton, who is reflective like Sarah, says of the scorpion applies to people like the Muirs as well: "Their skins are very sensitive to heat, which is why they live under stones and in holes and only come out a lot during the wet. If you build a ring of fire round them they're killed by the heat" (S 79).

The scorpion represents the members of the raj who shelter under outdated values. Those who maintain such values are consumed in the fires of history rather than silhouetted in the suffusive sunlight of past glories. So, Perron writes in his diary, days before the end of the raj on 6 August 1947, the anniversary of Hiroshima, how the day is closing "with the reflection of fires in the night sky" above Mirat. The past glories seem to characters like Perron, Sarah, and Mabel to have been only demonstrations of a misguided sense of superiority.[17]

The theme of the insects, and of their entrapment, is summed up by Barbie, who used to be "content to bear the burden of her own nature in the belief that God had known best what was right for her" (T 3) but who now cannot remember the principles that brought her to India. Barbie is no longer sure of the pattern of life, and she worries about human butterflies, caught in what Forster calls "the net Great Britain had thrown over India" (*Passage* 36). This is an extension of her previous concern for all those entangled in the once protective, now confining, shawl draped by God over a Christian world:[18] "Is the Universe an unprincipled design? Does God weep somewhere beyond it crying to its prisoners to free themselves and come to Him?" (T 199).

Scott views the fabric of the raj as itself an intricate cloth in which a series of characters are trapped, just as Barbie, using the christening shawl like a topee's veil, finds herself racing uncontrollably downhill caught in the midst of a thickening "nest of butterflies" (T 385).[19] There is a passage that Scott omitted from the final version of Barbie's descent, but which illustrates his aims well:

> Bounced by the tonga as it crossed an uneven junction of metalled and unmetalled road, [Barbie] feared ejection, automatically clung to the struts of the hood and then seemed held, transfixed, imprisoned like the butterflies, desiring escape but with no place to escape to because she had been woven into the web and did not exist outside it. Flutter as I may, she thought, I am stuck because a web however woven, by a visionary or a blind person, with good or bad intentions, is a web and remains so, until it is blown away, away, away.[20]

Whether scorched by the heat or blown away by the wind of a nuclear explosion, Scott's insects will find release from their imprisoning reality only in disaster—as Sarah says of the imprisoned scorpion, "it could never set about escaping without burning itself painfully to death" (S 80).

The end of the raj is seen by Scott as a crisis of faith akin to a loss in Christian belief. This ideological collapse leading to death is most fully explored in relation to Barbie, who comes to realise her failure in terms of "the unknown Indian," who is another kind of prisoner, epitomised by Hari Kumar. Barbie is a missionary teacher for whom the "teaching of reading, writing and arithmetic had never been as important as the teaching of Christianity" (T 4). Like Teddie's understanding of the raj, Barbie's view of the Christian mission is of a compelling doctrine that is unshakable; in its service one must sacrifice oneself and discipline others. However, while Teddie never realizes the shortcomings of *man-bap*, Barbie pointedly loses touch both with her principles and with the wisdom of her crusade in India. Scott represents Teddie's and Barbie's creeds as analogous. They are both ideologies that see their role as one of guidance and care: Teddie as mother and father to his men, Barbie as the shepherdess of her flock (she thinks Teddie "died in an attempt to gather strayed sheep into a fold" [T 269]). Their shared belief is

107

proclaimed in the hymn that the mission teaches to Indian children about a loving, caring God who will protect them:

> There's a Friend for little children
> Above the bright blue sky,
> A Friend Who never changes,
> Whose love will never die . . .   (J 15, 54)

The song gives a context to the "children" who later allow Teddie and Barbie to view themselves, and Jesus, in this parental way. It also illustrates the importance of Barbie's change of heart when she, unlike Teddie, comes to realize that there are alternatives to the Western foster-parents of *man-bap* and the mission: "Motherless, fatherless child. But it had Krishna as well as Jesus" (T 337).

So, how does Scott represent the recipients of this benevolence and the importance it has for the raj? According to Bakhtin, relationships are always a question of alterity because the individual's self-opinion is founded on his or her perception of the other and an awareness of the other's gaze (a simple point but one that is doubly significant when a way of life is partly based on "not seeing" particular groups of people):

> We evaluate ourselves from the standpoint of others, and through others we try to understand and take into account what is transgredient to our own consciousness. Thus, we take into account the value of our outward appearance from the standpoint of the possible impression it may produce upon the other.   (AA 15)

Neither physically nor mentally can individuals see themselves whole (without some kind of mirror), which is to say that a specular *other* is necessary to achieve a full perception of the self.[21] Also, everything that Bakhtin outlines with respect to the individual applies also to the group. A group is defined, and perceives itself, in relation to that which it finds outside itself. In other words, "parents" cannot exist or be understood without children, "prisoners" without jailers, or "the raj" without the colonized Indians it rules—and vice versa. Bakhtin again:

> To be means to be for the other, and through him, for oneself. Man has no internal sovereign territory; he is all and always on the boundary; looking within himself, he looks *in the eyes of the other* or *through the eyes of the other*. . . . I cannot become myself without the other; I must find myself in the other, finding the other in me (in mutual reflection and perception). Justification cannot be justification of *oneself*, confession cannot be confession of *oneself*. I receive my name from the other, and this name exists for the other.
> ("Towards a Reworking of the Dostoevsky Book," qtd. Todorov 96)

The designation received, though not always articulated, by the Indians in the *Quartet*, through their "other," the raj, is most nearly expressed in the title of the first section of the third novel: "The Unknown Indian." It is first explained when Barbie begins to see the picture of "The Jewel in Her Crown" in terms of this figure and its relation to her:

> When Barbie sat at her desk and gazed at the actual picture she was no longer sure of what she saw: Edwina guarding the body, Mabel kneeling to grub out weeds or inclining to gather roses; or herself, Barbie, surrounded by the children she had presumed to bring to God; or Miss Manners in some kind of unacceptable relationship with a man of another race whom she was intent on saving.
>
> From this there emerged a figure, the figure of an unknown Indian: dead in one aspect, alive in another. And after a while it occurred to her that the unknown Indian was what her life in India had been about. The notion alarmed her. She had not thought of it before in those terms and did not know what to do about it now that she had. She could not very well look for him because she did not know where to do that.   (T 69)

Barbie's perception of herself changes when she sees the allegorical picture of the hierarchy of the raj in another light. She realizes precisely that she needs to start to see, to "look for" Indians, though at this point she doesn't know where.The shift for her is from assuming God as the other in whose existence she sees herself reflected, to seeing, now that God will not enter into any dialogue with her, her worth in relation to the figure of the faceless Indian community around her. She now begins to think not only about the Indians she has taught but, through them, what "her life in India had been about." Barbie is led to a re-examination of herself and those like her. Bakhtin writes, in a strikingly Emersonian comment, "we are constantly and intently on the watch for reflections of our own life on the plane of other people's consciousness, and, more-over, not just reflections of particular moments of our life, but even reflections of the whole of it" (*AA* 16).

Scott's choice of the term "unknown Indian" is not hard to fathom. Nirad Chaudhuri's *The Autobiography of an Unknown Indian* is a classic work on the subject of Indo-British love-hate. Scott was certainly familiar with the book when he chose the name for his school teacher, Mr. Chaudhuri, and he built the image of the "unknown Indian" into each volume of the *Quartet* to describe the effect of the British presence in India, though he knew that the raj, like Barbie, seldom saw its role in such terms. This turning-point marks the conversion (parodied in the evangelical allusion in "the road to/from Dibrapur"[22]) that the pros-elytizer, Barbie, undergoes when she realizes the position of the "unknown Indian" and its reflection in/of her. One is defined by the other but only according to the status one accords to the other: if one sees the other as child, servant, or slave then the other's presence makes one a parent, employer, or master/mistress. The raj perceives Indians in these ways and so fails to see them as equal adult people. Consequently, the highest image it has of itself is fashioned from the pedagogic values of "guide and correct." One is reminded of Virginia Woolf's remark on the male self-image in *A Room of One's Own*:

> Women have served all these centuries as looking-glasses possessing the magic and delicious power of reflecting the figure of man at twice its natural size. Without that power probably the earth would still be swamp and jungle. . . . How is he to go on giving judgement, civilizing natives, making laws, writing books, dressing up and speechifying at banquets, unless he can see himself at breakfast and at dinner at least twice the size he really is? . . . The looking-glass vision is of supreme importance. . . .   (35-36)

Consonant with this view, Sister Ludmila remarks to the narrator at the end of her section in *The Jewel in the Crown*, "you are a curious people. In the main very conscious, as you walk in the sun, of the length or shortness of the shadows that you cast" (J 153).[23]

Barbie, in the quotation above, thinks of two Indians unknown to herself: one dead, Mr. Chaudhuri (referred to as "the unknown Indian" at T 297), and one alive, Hari. As she thinks about them her attitude to herself and the raj alters. This enactment is the fundamental corner-stone of the self for Bakhtin, beginning with the child-parent relationship:

> the question arises as to where I am to get the categories for fixing the self itself. The answer is: from other selves. I cannot see the self that is my own, so I must try to perceive it in others' eyes. This process of conceptually seeing myself by refracting the world through values of the other begins very early, when children first begin to see themselves through the eyes of the mother, and it continues all their lives.   (Clark and Holquist 73)

In this way, Barbie concludes that the raj has taught Indians to consider themselves "unknown." Most particularly, Scott describes how Hari, in common with the author of *The Autobiography of an Unknown Indian*, comes to perceive himself as nameless and unidentified. Scott also suggests that, in a curious way, the Anglo-Indians imagine the Indians invisible as individuals but present as a collective body for whom they must set an example; hence the sameness of two familiar idioms: "not in front of the children" and "not in front of the servants/natives." Scott shows this Indian anonymity under the raj throughout the *Quartet*:

"unknown Indian" is the term Sarah uses to describe whoever threw the stone that hit Teddie (S 163), while its plural is the only name that can be applied to the attackers on the road from Dibrapur and at the Bibighar. It is also Daphne's fear for Parvati, the human product of that night:

> Perhaps as the child grows, some likeness to Hari will become apparent. I so much hope so. Because that will be my vindication. I have nightmares of the child growing up to resemble no one, black-skinned, beyond redemption, a creature of the dark, a tiny living mirror of that awful night. And yet, even so, it will be a child. A god-given creature, if there is a god, . . . deserving of that portion of our blessing we can spare.   (J 365)[24]

In addition to these figures, there are also the many unknown Indians who help Barbie (as they helped Sister Ludmila) and so add to her consciousness of the raj's failure to recognise the equal humanity of Indians and its consequent perception of itself as superhuman or god-like. Barbie's realization of this failure is the worthy side to her "apotheosis" which would otherwise seem ironic (Scott's early title for *The Towers of Silence* was "The Apotheosis of Barbara Batchelor"—the most explicit reference in the completed novel is Barbie's longing for an "apotheosis" like Edwina Crane's [T 65].)[25] In other words, Barbie starts to perceive what was beyond or left out of the monologic, centripetal ideology of the raj and her own endeavours in India: the previously invisible Indian.

Just as the British are, in a sense, as imprisoned as Hari and MAK, it is also clear that the figure of the "unknown Indian" is a reflection of the image of these prisoners. At one point, Barbie, talking to an Indian orphan, recalls the blind lacemaker's words—"*Ah, oui, pauvre papillon. C'est un de mes prisonniers*" (S 356)—and she combines the image of the prisoner with that of the unknown Indian. She does this under the auspices of *man-bap*, in her conversation with Ashok:

> "What am I?" she asked Ashok.
> "You are Sahib-log."
> "No, I am a servant of the Lord Jesus."
> She sat on the verandah steps of the rectory bungalow and offered her hand. Ashok looked at her seriously.
> "Come," she said "I am your father and your mother."
> He came. She clasped his thin shoulders.
> "You don't understand," she said in English. He smelt musky. "It is all too long ago and far away. The world you and I live in is corrupt. I clasp you to my breast but you conceive of this in terms of an authority unbending. I offer my

love. You accept it as a sign of fortune smiling. Your heart beats with gratitude, excitement, expectation of rupees. And mine scarcely beats at all. It is very tired and old and far from home. Ashoka, Ashoka, Shokam, Shokarum, Shokis, Shokis." Somewhere she had got that wrong. . . .

She put a silver rupee into his tiny hand. He salaamed and ran. At the gate he turned. They waved to each other.

"Tu es mon petit Hindou inconnu," she whispered. "Et tu es un papillon brun. Moi, je suis blanche. Mais nous sommes les prisonniers du bon Dieu."

(T 359)

The symbol used for the raj's failure here, and it is common to many scenes in the four novels, is that of reaching out to others—holding them and touching hands. Ashok, Barbie decides, is a *Hari*jan, an untouchable child of God, but she reaches out to him lovingly with her hand, makes contact, and in time is rewarded with his friendship when he says he will go to Rajputana only if she goes with him.[26] The image is also there in Edwina Crane at the roadside holding Mr. Chaudhuri's hand; in Hari and Daphne's hand-holding after they are attacked; and lastly in Merrick's inability to reach out and touch others, which Scott later symbolizes in the loss of Merrick's arm.[27] The inability to make contact is the "failure to unify" which forms Scott's diagnosis of the sickness at the heart of the raj. An example of this occurs at Mirat station when an Indian woman pushes her way towards the Laytons' wedding-party and pleads for her nephew on her knees. Hari's Aunt Shalini is of course unrecognised by all around her (except Merrick) and so she is ignored: "It could be assumed that the woman was known: a poor, mad, harmless creature who pestered sahibs" (S 207). In fact, she is "unknown" and like the harijan Ashok "it was impossible to touch her" (S 206). She is hurried away by an Indian official.

This failure to reach out accounts for an absence in the picture that appears in the hands of Edwina, Sarah, Merrick, and Barbie, who passes it around among the unreceptive memsahibs. Barbie says that the unknown Indian is important to "The Jewel in Her Crown" precisely because "he" is missing:

> "One should always share one's hopes," she said. "That represents one of the unfulfilled ones. Oh, not the gold and scarlet uniforms, not the pomp, not the obeisance. We've had all that and plenty. We've had everything in the picture except what got left out."
>
> "What was that, Miss Batchelor?"
>
> She said, not wishing to use that emotive word, "I call it the unknown Indian. He isn't *there*. So the picture isn't finished." (T 382-83)

The unknown Indian isn't there because he is generally unseen by the raj: "I am invisible, Kumar said, not only to white people because they are white and I am black but invisible to my white friend because he can no longer distinguish me in a crowd" (J 262).

The emotive word that Barbie does not wish to mention is of course "love" (the love that defines a power for unity: Daphne's love for Hari, Lady Manners's for Parvati. It is also present to a lesser degree in Sarah's affection for Ahmed, Miss Crane's for Mr. Chaudhuri, Barbie's for Ashok). This is a word which Barbie cannot use in front of Merrick but can murmur to the *chokra* Ashok: "I offer love. You accept it as a sign of fortune smiling." Love, though present in the rhetoric of songs like "There's a Friend for little children," is that which Barbie, and Scott, feels has been absent from the raj's "smugly pious" picture of itself (J 21). Barbie's conversion, like Edwina Crane's, means turning away from a distant God and towards people who have previously been unknown and invisible. Barbie realizes that she can only make known the invisible Indian through love, as Lacan argues: "I can only just prove to the Other that he exists, not, of course, with the proofs for the existence of God, with which over the centuries he has been killed off, but by loving him" (*Ecrits* 317).

To conclude this chapter where it began, an identity has to be constructed for the unknown Indian. At one point, Barbie chooses that of "Daphne Manners's Indian boyfriend," but of course his name remains unknown to her (T 72). For the reader also, returning always to the Bibighar, the unknown Indian must be "Hari." But, because his figure is half-formed by England, it is also "Harry." To go beyond this dichotomy, there is the name he gives to himself and which represents all the outcasts and prisoners in the novels, who are for Scott all half-Indian and half-English: Philoctetes. Hari selects this name to suit the reflection of himself he sees in the eyes of the raj. There are several reasons (some are Scott's, some are Hari's). First, Philoctetes possessed the bow and arrows needed to take Troy and therefore is linked with Apollo, "The lord of the unerring bow" (Byron, "Childe Harold," iv, 161):

Apparently her other name was Daphne which for those who still remembered snippets of classical mythology produced the image of a girl running from the embrace of the sun god Apollo, her limbs and streaming hair already delineating the arboreal form in which her chastity would be preserved, enshrined forever; forever green. From her, then, the god could pluck no more than leaves. (T 59)

But, as Daphne realizes, her name is another illusion of the raj, and its associations seem ironic (not least because our first image of her running from Hari is to save him, not herself):

> If it is a boy, please name him Harry, or Hari, if his skin is dark enough to *honour* that kind of spelling. If a girl . . . please *don't* call her Daphne. That's the girl who ran from Apollo, and was changed into a laurel bush! With me it's been the other way round, hasn't it? Rooted clumsily in the earth, thinking I'm running free, chasing the sun-god . . . because being tall I had an idea that I was a sort of graceful Diana type — long-legged and slender, taut as a bow, flitting through the forest!   (J 365)

In terms of Hindu mythology, Daphne does not run away from Hari, another name for Visnu, but from Siva, represented by her attackers. It is Siva, God of the lingam and of cosmic destruction that Daphne dreams of, and it is he who carries the Pinaka bow and the celestial arrows. In this mythology, it is Siva who marries Parvati; and the two of them engender the newly created world:

> Another level of sexual antagonism exists between Siva and Parvati . . . as God of the phallus, and as her husband, he is forced to make love to her and, ultimately, to produce a child. . . . Siva is man and Parvati is woman: they are the causes of creation. All men have Siva as their soul, and all women Parvati.[28]

As noted in chapter 2, Scott mixes mythologies to produce an image of the confusion of "separate destinies" that the raj's involvement in the subcontinent represents. In Indian terms, the night of the Bibighar for Daphne is a night of contraries: of pursuit (by Merrick) and flight (from Hari); of a lover and a band of attackers; of Visnu and Siva; of creation and destruction, love and rape, giving and taking.[29]

The second reason for Hari's choosing the name Philoctetes is that the Greek archer was abandoned on the island of Lemnos by Odysseus and his shipmates. He was made an outcast because of an ugly, festering foot wound (the same stigma attaches to Hari's skin colour) from either a snake-bite — another reason for Scott to compare Merrick to the snake — or one of Herakles's poisoned arrows (see D 550). Hence, Philoctetes, like Hari, was rejected by those he trusted and took to be his friends. In Hari's case, he is wounded by the raj, by the sting of the scorpion which, like the bite of the snake to which Scott (e.g., S 78) often relates it, leaves a spreading poison in a gaping wound.[30]

Finally, Scott may have given Hari his Greek name because Philoctetes lit Herakles's funeral pyre. This act by his chosen namesake associates

114

Hari with suttee and with the fires that surround so many of the prisoners throughout the *Quartet,* though it is the position of stranded outcast that directly signifies Hari's isolation and confinement.

Through its illustrative use of Philoctetes's offending skin, the *Quartet* again reinforces Scott's belief that racial prejudice is the key social and moral evil of his day (M 145). In a book review, he quoted the opinion of a Western-educated son of a Bengali Brahmin—words which clearly endorse Scott's characterization of Hari:

> The deepest tragedy of British Rule in India is that it succeeded in producing individuals like me who can neither feel an identity with their own people nor accept . . . the West. We are left crying in the wilderness and are forced to adopt the horrifying vulgarity of the stranded pose.[31]

So, Hari leaves prison as Philoctetes leaves Lemnos: "The exile will, indeed, return to the community, but here is no romance, no hope for virtue to live 'happily ever after.' This is a tragic figure, for whom heaven has ordained, in promised happiness, enduring sorrow."[32] Hari is an islanded exile, and in this respect he is associated with all the characters in the book who are either imprisoned or outcast by society. On the one hand, he chooses exile as the same humble escape into anonymity that his grandfather chose in going *sannyasi.* On the other hand, he now becomes an embodiment of the image that the raj has made its other:

> To characterize a person, group, or institution as "other" is to place them outside the system of normality or convention to which one belongs oneself. Such processes of exclusion by categorization are thus central to certain ideological mechanisms. . . . If members of a given racial group are collectively seen as other, then how they are treated is irrelevant to what humanity demands. . . . What lies behind use of this term is the perception that when we divide reality up into separate components these are typically seen in a sort of figure-ground manner, with one component representing a norm and other components representing divergences from this norm.
>
> (Hawthorn 124)

Race, class, sex, religion, and nationality are barriers raised before many of the characters in the *Quartet* to create the figure-ground positions of self and other. As Francine Weinbaum (1978, 104) has noted, the major characters of the novels attempt to break through many kinds of barriers in attempts to find union. And Scott once wrote that several of the novels' major images are precisely of individuals outside "the closed safe little circle of [their] own kind" (M 66). This also applies to those who, otherwise accepted, become stranded when they link themselves with the victims of bigotry. When Daphne decides

115

to protect Hari, she realizes that she too must become an outcast: "I didn't dare tell the truth so the only thing I could do was to confuse and puzzle people and make them hate me" (J 417). Sarah, the character with the strongest sense of exile and the least sympathy for the raj's perception of itself, also creates a sense of her own difference through her willingness to know Indians and to feel their presence. Barbie realizes this in Sarah's reaction to the character who is himself most willing to act out the raj's contempt for Hari and all who are outcast: Merrick.

> "You didn't like him."
> After a while Sarah shook her head.
> "No. I don't think I liked him at all."
> Perhaps, Barbie thought, because you had seen the child and talked to the old woman, and had seen the other woman, the woman in the white saree, and felt the presence of the unknown Indian.   (T 176)

In Scott's symbolic structure, Sarah is not one of the unknown but one of the toughened "butterflies." She is related to Hari, however, through Scott's picture of the common plight of exiles and their shared sense of isolation and division. Sarah feels cut-off, alone and in need of recovery. Because she feels she is always on show and without a private life, anything personal reminds her of her exile, like a "message in a bottle cast back up by an indifferent tide on an island on which she sometimes felt herself the only one alive who still wanted to be rescued" (S 140). Sarah recognizes her positions as exile and prisoner, but she is able to return "home" to evolve her new identity among "the people we really are." This is what connects her to, yet divides her from, Hari: he also forges a new identity, but, as a still unrescued Philoctetes, he is left behind once more while the raj sails home.[33]

CHAPTER SEVEN

Engaging with the Situation

> This was the first of a string of coincidences which linked what happened to the Laytons to the unsavoury affair of the Manners girl. Retrospectively, it seemed that a malign influence, loosed by that affair, and searching for another victim, a house to haunt, arbitrarily and unfairly, but perhaps significantly selected a family whose history had been such as set an example to Anglo-India of dutiful service and correct living.
>
> *(The Towers of Silence,* unpublished draft) [1]

This chapter concentrates on the only figure who has a substantial role in every volume of the *Quartet*: Ronald Merrick. He is the embodiment of the "malign influence" mentioned above. He "selects" the Laytons because they signify everything he has been taught to reverence and has learned to resent. Merrick also becomes a "victim" of his own acceptance of the raj legend and his theory of contempt and envy. He formulates and applies this theory in terms of the relationship between the raj and Indians; yet it is *his* envy, occasioned by an over-awareness of humble origins and his few social graces, that spurs him on to become a part of the myth of upper-class Anglo-India.

In Merrick's story self-destruction is occasioned by his hate for everything that another part of himself desires — this is an extreme example of the kind of simultaneous attraction and repulsion that Homi Bhabha in his early work positions at the heart of colonial subjectivity. [2] With Hari, Merrick has an ambivalent fascination which nearly destroys him, and then, with Aziz, he develops an infatuation which brings his inevitable defeat; on the first occasion he resorts to violence to punish Hari, Daphne, and his own attraction to both of them, but on the second he succumbs to his repressed desires and makes love to an "inferior," dark-skinned, Indian boy. [3] Every one of Merrick's prescribed lines is transgressed: race, class, colour, sex, and authority. Consequently, he can no longer sustain the ambition and self-belief that drive his life. Yet, before power and desire overwhelm him, Merrick has, as Perron notes, managed to displace his self-loathing: "Self-punishment being out of the question, Merrick punished the men he chose. After Karim Muzzafir Khan's suicide I was never in any doubt about Merrick's repressed homosexuality" (D 302).

Scott ensures that Merrick's influence is seen to be symptomatic of the "dark forces" in the novels and in history. The meeting between Hari and Merrick is one instance of a more general trend, one in which the figure of the unknown Indian is indicative of an attitude of history:

> Place Merrick at home, in England, and Harry Coomer abroad, in England, and it is Coomer on whom the historian's eye lovingly falls; he is a symbol of our virtue. In England it is Merrick who is invisible. Place them there, in India, and the historian cannot see either of them. They have wandered off the guideline, into the jungle. But throw a spotlight on them and it is Merrick on whom it falls. There he is, the unrecorded man, one of the kind of men we really are (as Sarah would say). Yes, their meeting was logical. And they had met before, countless times.   (D 302)

To reinforce their exemplary status, Scott confers on his two dark men two dark archetypes, immortal forms of darkness: "Hari" in Hindu mythology is a form of krishna, "the dark one,"[4] and Merrick is frequently associated with Satan (Barbie says explicitly that Merrick is the devil [D 375]).

To expand on the kind of archetypes involved in the meeting between Hari and Marrick, I need now to turn to Sartre and his account of human relations and of colonialism. In *Heart of Darkness* Marlow famously says that "The conquest of the earth . . . is not a pretty thing when you look into it too much" (10). Sixty years after Conrad's novel, Sartre, in the introduction to Fanon's plangently anti-colonialist book *The Wretched of the Earth*, writes in similar terms about humanism: "There you can see it, quite naked, and it's not a pretty sight. It was nothing but an ideology of lies, a perfect justification for pillage; its honeyed words, its affectation of sensibility were only alibis for our aggressions" (21). Sartre explicitly identifies his audience as the European colonialists that Fanon's book accuses. His is the same general audience as Marlow's on the "Nellie," and the first-person pronoun of "our aggressions" refers to the same breed of rapacious colonialists deplored by Marlow. But for Sartre there is no redeeming idea at the back of the greed and aggression, no significant division between those who "go at it blind" and those who, he believes, condone the idea of colonialism through their assumption of Western superiority—an assumption founded on a belief in human moral progress.[5] To Sartre it is the idea of humanism itself that is "not a pretty thing." What interests Scott here, is the question of what would replace humanism as a basis for moral action, since he does not see humanism as irreparably compromised by history, as Sartre does.

Though drunk, Perron manages to explain Scott's definition of the paternalism that Sartre allies with humanism:

> that Kiplingesque double-talk that transformed India from a place where plain ordinary greedy Englishmen carved something out for themselves to balance out the more tedious consequences of the law of primogeniture, into one where they appeared to go voluntarily into exile for the good of their souls and the uplift of the native.   (D 209)

It is against this that Scott places *his* conception of humanism. I noted earlier that Scott says that he writes about the raj because the death and interment of liberal humanism is still a living issue for him. By liberal humanism he says he means "dignity." In opposition to this belief, he places Merrick, who is not simply a latter-day paternalistic imperialist but also an exponent of basic aspects of Sartre's philosophy. Scott, writing in the sixties and early seventies, places a character like Merrick, embodying some of Sartre's existentialist ideas about the human predicament, against his representatives of humanism—Sarah, Lady Manners, and Mabel Layton. Scott's conclusion is that, in his understanding of the term, humanism, despite its faults, is preferable to Sartre's alternative.

In the key to special terminology appended to her translation of *Being and Nothingness*, Hazel Barnes explains that Sartre's verb *engager* includes "both the idea of involvement and the idea of deliberate commitment" (631). In one of his essays, Scott describes *engagement* as "discovering and working within your unique historical situation" (M 131). Now, although he does not use the specific word *engagement*, these are also the broad terms in which Merrick outlines his own theories. To begin with, the concept of *engagement* parallels his belief in acting out relationships in accordance with one's position in the social hierarchy. While Merrick's views are propounded on many different occasions throughout the *Quartet*, there is each time a stress on the need to make things happen, on the need to be engaged. He tells Sarah, "you ought to be able to act, you ought to be involved. As an individual" (S 213). Again, demonstrating a belief in engaging with the world, he asserts to Hari, "The ideas, without the enactment, lose their significance" (S 297). Therefore, in order to comprehend his behaviour, it is necessary to outline his beliefs, which fall into three areas: the theories of drawing the line, the "situation," and contempt and envy. I shall examine them in turn, and consider Sartre's connections with each.

One of Merrick's habits is "drawing the line" in order to establish moral boundaries, but for Scott such demarcations only promote division and simplification while denying the right to individuality. Merrick explains his belief in relation to Daphne's friendship with Hari:

> She didn't see why a line had to be drawn—has to be drawn. But it's essential, isn't it? You have to draw a line. Well, it's arbitrary. Nine times out of ten perhaps you draw it in the wrong place. But you need it there, you need to be able to say: There's the line. This side of it is right. That side is wrong. Then you have your moral term of reference. Then you can act. You can feel committed. You can be involved. Your life takes on something like a shape. It has form. Purpose as well, maybe. You know who you are when you wake up in the morning. Well sometimes you can rub the line out and draw it in a different place, bring it closer or push it farther out. But you need it there. It's like a blind man with a white stick needing the edge of the pavement.
>
> (S 214-15)

This is Merrick's starting-point for action; and action for Sartre is crucial if one is not to be inauthentic, not to be guilty of trying to escape one's existence in the world. Importantly, Merrick's lines can be redrawn and are not mere substitutes for decision-making, but sincere beliefs that he wishes to embrace and enforce. In contrast to this position, Scott presents characters such as Perron, who are neither actively engaged nor committed, but who are contemplative, questioning, and sensitive in attempting to understand the complexities of history that have led to the current state of affairs. For Scott, the *necessity* of commitment would be dangerously suggestive of Dyer and Amritsar as well as Merrick and the Bibighar.[6]

Conversely, for Merrick, Hari is responsible for the Bibighar—"If you were a hundred miles away you'd still be responsible" (S 298)—and so are all "liberal intellectuals" because they do not acknowledge the "lines" or their necessity. Merrick tells Daphne that colour "matters like hell" (J 391), while Lady Manners observes, echoing Daphne, that it is only "the last division of all" (J 448). Lady Manners's statement is a sad comment about attitudes like Merrick's—she is one of the liberals who feel dismayed because the division, the line-drawing, persists.

It is to line-drawing that one owes the worst prejudices of racism, since skin-colour is such an elementary example of difference. Merrick believes it to be a necessary distinction, derived from a true superiority:

> The Indians themselves have this prejudice about paleness. To them a fair skin denotes descent from the civilized Aryan invaders from the north, a black skin descent from the primitive aboriginals who were pushed into the jungles and hills, or fled south. There is this connotation that paleness has of

something more finely, more delicately adjusted. Well—superior. Capable of leading. Equipped mentally and physically to dominate.   (S 217)

Teddie is always a useful character to measure Merrick against, and they share a belief in line-drawing. However, Teddie's response to Merrick's assertion of the importance of boundaries reveals both a significant discrepancy between them and also why Merrick is so dangerous. Teddie replies, "The line's already there, isn't it? We don't have to draw it" (T 147). To Teddie, the lines are simply given: patriotism, *man-bap*, social classes, good manners, rules and regulations. For Merrick, these are matters over which he can, and to be engaged he must, exercise his own will. Merrick is thus able to indulge his personal grievances, and in doing so believes he is legitimately realizing the forces at work in his own restructuring of those hierarchies that Teddie takes for granted. This is what Merrick calls acting out "the situation" (Teddie, who doesn't draw his own lines, is of course baffled by Merrick's reference to "situations" [T 148]). Most of what Merrick believes about the "situation" is revealed by Hari:

> history was a sum of situations whose significance was never seen until long afterwards because people had been afraid to act them out. They couldn't face up to their responsibility for them. They preferred to think of the situations they found themselves in as part of a general drift of events.
>
> (S 297)

Again, the expression "the situation" is a particular one for Sartre. Hazel Barnes gives the following gloss: "The For-itself's *engagement* in the world. It is the product of both facticity and the For-itself's way of accepting and acting upon its facticity." The For-itself is, roughly, Sartre's term for consciousness; facticity is the contingent circumstance of the For-itself's necessary connection with the world, with all that is other than itself, via the body. Facticity therefore includes one's sex, parents, race, and appearance plus the broad social, historical, and financial conditions of one's particular existence. Merrick's use of the term "situation" expresses his involvement in the conjunctures of the *Quartet*—it is the product of his personal, social, and professional circumstances and relationships plus his method of "accepting and acting upon" them.

Sartre devotes a little over a tenth of *Being and Nothingness* to a discussion of "Freedom and Facticity: The Situation."[7] Its import for us can be summed up as follows:

man is defined first of all as a being "in a situation." That means that he forms a synthetic whole with his situation — biological, economic, political, cultural, etc. He cannot be distinguished from his situation, for it forms him and decides his possibilities; but, inversely, it is he who gives it meaning by making his choices within it and by it. To be in a situation, as we see it, is to choose oneself in a situation, and men differ from one another in their situations and also in the choices they themselves make of themselves. What men have in common is not a "nature" but a condition, that is, an ensemble of limits and restrictions: the inevitability of death, the necessity of working for a living, of living in a world already inhabited by other men.

Fundamentally this condition is nothing more than the basic human situation, or, if you prefer, the ensemble of abstract characteristics common to all situations.   (Sartre, qtd. Natanson 57)[8]

The importance of the "situation" in the *Quartet* is that it mirrors the general facts of British rule in India. Merrick is in charge of Hari, has taken him into his power, and is now free to act as he sees fit. In order to be true to the reality of the world, of Britain's rule of India, Merrick believes he must enact the "master and man situation" (D 313). In the Mayapore police headquarters, he is able to exploit his position of authority for the investigation into Daphne's rape, and circumstances allow him both to explain and enact his theory of contempt and envy before Hari. According to Sartre, such an enactment is crucial because the relation of a For-itself to a situation is realized only by acting out an aspect of the situation that the For-itself chooses to engage (Natanson 50). In Merrick's case this amounts to acting out Hari's subservience to him — based on racial, institutional, and circumstantial factors. However, these are combined with Merrick's own views on the relation of the individual to the other.

His theory of human relationships hinges on a belief that individuals are motivated by contempt and envy. Contempt is also the word used by Fanon in his formulation of humanism's invitation to subject peoples to imitate Western values: "Western bourgeois racial prejudice as regards the nigger and the Arab is a racism of contempt" because it proclaims "mankind's outstanding dignity" and "an essential equality between men" while "inviting the sub-men to become human, and to take as their prototype Western humanity as incarnated in the Western bourgeoisie" (Fanon 131). On this analysis, Merrick agrees with Fanon and acts out the "truth" of his argument. Theoretically, he persecutes Hari because, while Hari has been allowed to become "fully human," Merrick believes he is still really despised by the British because his skin-colour means he is genetically one of the "sub-men." Merrick's theory of contempt and its ramifications for action rely on two key points: "knowing oneself superior to all other races especially black and having a duty to guide and correct them" (D 209). This to Merrick is the truth of the raj and it is the "situation" with which he becomes fully engaged. Others, he believes, have "guided" Hari, helped him to try to become "fully human" by giving him a Western education. Now, the necessity also to "correct" means that *man-bap* must be run on a principle of punishment, not forgiveness—Merrick's "lash of anger" and not Teddie's "tears of sorrow" (D 209).

However, in his treatment of Hari there is as much envy as contempt and this introduces the personal side of his victimization of Hari as a particular, chosen individual.[9] Merrick is openly envious of Hari's education and accent, of his marks of "superiority" in terms of class. As he makes Hari palpably aware, Merrick has been exposed to barriers of class, and he transposes these into a general view of a common human predicament governed by basic feelings of superiority and inferiority:

> In India he'd got on far better than he could have done at home. In India he automatically became a Sahib. He hobnobbed on equal terms with people who would snub him at home and knew they would snub him. When he considered all the things that made him one of them in India—colonial solidarity, equality of position, the wearing of a uniform, service to king and country—he knew that these were fake. They didn't fool either him or the middle and upper class people he hobnobbed with. What they had in common was the contempt they all felt for the native race of the country they ruled.   (S 299-300)

Merrick's views are therefore based on hierarchies, on sharply drawn divisions of superiority and inferiority. He not only believes in his superiority to Hari and the necessity to play out that fact, but he also thinks that the racial hierarchy ought to be realized and enacted. He thinks himself inferior to, and so is envious of, anyone with social status. Again, this is a criticism of the ideology of British humanism which argues that everyone is equal but, because of the class system, treats individuals differently. He is reported to have given the example of himself and an upper-class Englishman in a room thinking themselves superior to an Indian.

> then if the Indian left the room the understanding would subtly change. [Merrick] was then the inferior man. He said you couldn't buck this issue, that relationships between people were based on contempt, not love, and that contempt was the prime human emotion because no human being was ever going to believe all human beings were born equal. If there was an

emotion almost as strong as contempt it was envy. He said a man's personality existed at the point of equilibrium between the degree of his envy and the degree of his contempt.   (S 300)

This view that contempt and envy, rather than love, drives relationships is also reflected in Sartre's pessimistic view of humanity, in which "human reality is not originally communal but, rather, is in conflict—in necessary and perpetual conflict" (Natanson 47). Similarly, the primary purpose of sexual encounter for Sartre is power over the other. This is certainly the nature of Merrick's sexual toying with Hari, in which Hari is naked, trussed up, fondled, and sexually provoked and humiliated alternately. For Sartre, "love" has two aspects—one masochistic (being treated like an object) and one sadistic (treating another as an object). These are mirrored in Merrick's extremes of envy (considering oneself inferior) and contempt (considering oneself superior) which similarly allow no room for communality, but compel relationships toward disharmony, dominance, and subservience. Solomon expresses Sartre's view thus:

> Sartre allows that our "first attitude" towards the other is that of love. But the attempt at love is essentially abortive, for the primitive structure of every human relation is already based on the other's attempts to treat me as an object in his eyes . . . love of an other is *possession* of that other.
>
> (Solomon 312)

Merrick's attraction to Hari is, of course, expressed as a desire to possess and hold sway over him, just as Britain possesses and controls India. Power is also what drives him to have Perron transferred under his command and to steal Susan's psychiatric records; in both circumstances he can feel contempt for someone he would otherwise envy.

From this outline of Merrick, Scott's hostility to Sartre's ideas (see M 131) can be comprehended. This is not least because love is Scott's prime force in the *Quartet*.[10] To him, the attitudes represented by Merrick only serve to debase the real feelings of love that lie behind others' good actions: sacrifice, sympathy, charity, kindness, and forgiveness.

It must also be noted that Merrick's beliefs are self-fulfilling: he thinks that relationships are founded on contempt and envy, and so tries to ensure that his relationships with people exist at that level. In contrast, Scott uses other characters (Sarah, Barbie, Daphne) to stress human individuality and the unique qualities of circumstances and the people within them; for him there is no "situation" as such. To Merrick, this is liberal hypocrisy because it pretends to ignore the power relationships that really dictate our feelings towards others ("The liberal intellectual Englishman was just as contemptuous of the Westernized educated Indian as the arrogant upper-class reactionary Englishman was of the fellow who blacks his boots and earns his praise" [S 299]).

So far, I have examined one view of Merrick—the perspective gained from an examination of his own beliefs about human emotions and relationships. To understand Scott's characterization of him more fully I want now to put his theories in a wider context, that of his self-construction and his destruction:

> "Even that arm, you know, is an invention. You needn't think it happened in a flash, with a bang, or even on an operating table. It appeared quite gradually, like the stigmata on a saint's hands and feet and side. So that the world would notice."   (Perron, D 205)

> "He is one of your hollow men. The outer casing is almost perfect and he carried it off almost to perfection. But, of course, it is a casing he has designed. This loss he has sustained—the left arm—even this fits. . . . I am tempted to say that had he not suffered the loss he might one day have been forced to invent it."   (Bronowsky, D 171)

From the opening book, Merrick is an outsider. Daphne is the person he first chooses to marry, but for her he is only "a dark shadow, just on the edge of my life" (J 379). He becomes emotionally close to no one but affects almost everyone, finding in numerous men and women something that he wishes to implant or excoriate in himself. It is not until he can exploit the mental weakness of Susan Layton that his cloak of darkness, his coldness and toughness, is generally accepted as a shield of protection and reliability. He has the traditional qualities endorsed by the raj but none of the caring sentiments that, in the eyes of a figure like John Layton, accompany them. Merrick is not permanently on show in quite the same way as other characters—his disguises and subterfuges prevent this—but he lacks an inner, personal world because he is always presented in the narrative from the outside. The reader never enters his thoughts and though this could be considered a fault in the novels, it does emphasize Bronowsky's comment above, that Merrick is a "hollow" man, a man of externalities and coverings. On those few occasions when the reader encounters him in a private moment he seems to be looking outward not inward, as when Barbie finds him at Rose cottage: "gazing as from a height, upon a world spread out before him" (T 370).[11] Merrick models himself on public images, and so the only people to accept him on a private level are those who have little inner life or understanding themselves: Susan, Teddie, their child, and arguably

125

Mildred. For a character such as Perron, his effect is entirely different. Perron talks of "Merrick's passionate exploration outwards from the hollow centre of his self-invented personality . . . and of his profound contempt for anything, for anybody, that crumbled without resisting" (D 230). He sees Merrick as a man who, persecuted for any inadequacy, has made himself emotionless and efficient—with the result that, exuding both "a gratitude and a contempt" (D 231), he scorns and exploits any weakness in others.

Works on colonialism are inevitably infused with a discourse surrounding the presentation of stereotypes, and I will now say something about this discourse before returning to see how it reflects on Merrick.[12] It is a common observation that the colonialist apprehends who he or she is primarily through a stress on distinctions from those who are colonized; however, as Holquist (1989, 207) has pointed out, from Bakhtin's theory of dialogism, stereotyping (a process which seeks to fix, objectify and harden the image of the other and maintain a "finished-off quality of the image it produces"[13]) is an activity which all persons participate in all the time with regard to one another. Stereotyping is an inevitable consequence of the temporal and spatial conditions of perception because "the subject seeks to finalize the other in a fixed identity" which can govern the subject's actions with regard to that other (209). Individuals necessarily categorize (and so fix or stereotype) others in a way that they do not categorize themselves because the self is always perceived to be in perpetual development—the individual is dynamic—while others have to be objects of consciousness which are thought of in terms of the individual's finished ideational version of them—they are static. Individuals see themselves as open to the future and therefore do not need to label themselves, to encode themselves in language, as they do those who are external to them. Our perception of others can only be updated sporadically through contact or reflective identification.

Bakhtin argues that the relation of self to other is similar to that between author and character—the author is open to the future, aware of thought-processes and consciousness, decisions, choices, and possibilities, but the character is animated only when an identification of author with character takes place. The author is aware of moving through time whereas the characters exist only in the past, when written about, or in the present, when identified with. Spatially, others are held as objects of the individual's senses, and are compared or assessed from a specific and unique point of addressivity; temporally, individuals are aware only of their own movement through time, a time which others intersect but never run parallel with. The position of being inside themselves specifically distinguishes each individual from those who are outside and who are therefore given defining, totalizing qualities of which some of the most obvious are nationality, accent, social class, gender, and race.[14]

However, the relation of self to other becomes more significant when individuals attempt to approach themselves in this closed, finished way, as Merrick does. In order to view the self to such a degree that it is stereotyped, individuals have to be looking habitually for impressions made on others and to be dismissive of their, necessarily different, perception of their own presence. The individual has to be, in terms of Merrick and the *Quartet*, externally oriented and inwardly "hollow." According to Holquist, Bakhtin argues that a construction of the self cannot be achieved without the other: "it is only the other's categories that will allow me to be an object for my own perception. I see my self as I conceive others might see it. In order to forge a self, I must do so from *outside*. In other words, I *author myself*" (Holquist, *Dialogism* 28). For each individual, the immediate reality of his or her own living particularity, a uniqueness that presents itself as only for the individual, is a shared event with pre-existing external reality. This dialogue, however, can be heavily biased and accented.

That is, Merrick presents himself in such a way that the reflection of himself he sees in others conforms to the idealized and finalized simulacrum of a dependable, strict, unshakable, successful officer of the raj—which is an image he has learned from the myths of his youth.[15] All sides of his self that fail to conform to this "front" will be hidden or repressed in order that the outside image is preserved intact. He identifies himself with this image despite, if not indeed because of, his lack of the social background and privileges that usually accompany that image. Paradoxically, he wishes to join and epitomize a ruling class he has always been encouraged to feel acutely different from.[16] Colonel Layton identifies this effect as follows:

> "I suppose you can say India's made him what he is, but after all isn't it India that's given *us* whatever distinction we have? . . . India's always been an opportunity for quite ordinary English people—it's given us the chance to live and work like, well, a ruling class that few of us could really claim to belong to." (D 370)

Perron says that Merrick has been duped by theories of the White Man's Burden—to guide and correct other peoples. Because of his own background, Merrick is susceptible to any such picture of the world graded according to social strata (where the superior groups rule and discipline the inferior—rather than simply exploiting their material resources and labour). Perron therefore also sees the raj, and in particular Merrick's self-invention, in terms of class. Merrick has been taken in by the rhetoric that transformed upper-class greed into the burden to guide and correct:

> The transformation was illusory of course. A middle-class misconception of upper-class *mores*. But a man like Merrick can't be expected to see that. He's spent too long inventing himself in the image to have energy left to realize that as an image it is and always was hollow. He only notices it has become rarer.   (D 209)

Merrick's identities shift as he moves toward his ambition, and in the tetralogy he is given at least three alternative roles. In the first novel he is Daphne's White Robot; in the third he becomes Barbie's Prince of Darkness; and in the last, Count Dracula: inhuman figures of the automaton, the devil, and the living dead. Merrick's denial of his previous identities is his defining feature—his homosexuality is closeted, his past at Mayapore, like the deleterious childhood experiences he tries to outgrow, is covered over; and finally his own body, his arm and face, is made artificial. However, all along, Merrick is dogged by reminders of the Bibighar, physical messages that tell him he won't be allowed to forget, that he cannot escape from who he has been in the past.

At each stage of his self-invention (as he acquires the qualities of efficient DSP, dutiful best man, INA expert, understanding suitor, caring father) he seems to appear from nowhere, evincing those characteristics that are needed to succeed in his present objective. Merrick does not evolve, but mutates into the necessary form for his new role. As he does this he tries to sew a seamless personality together, a closed self that is neither changing nor other than he wills it to be. What he fails to acknowledge is his own multi-sidedness, considering each of his incarnations fixed. Bakhtin writes:

> A man never coincides with himself. One cannot apply the formula of identity A = A. . . . [T]he genuine life of the personality takes place at the point of noncoincidence between a man and himself, at his point of departure beyond the limits of all that he is as a material being, a being that can be spied on, defined. . . .   (*PDP* 59)

Merrick refuses this openness and lack of definition, wishing instead to identify himself completely with his self-image, in the way that an individual can identify someone else as a finished, closed image. He expunges all traces of dialogue within himself, to emerge monolithic, coalescent, and unfragmented. So, in the narrative, Merrick always arrives ready-made for his new role. At Mirat he is unseen by Teddie for several days, while Teddie wonders who "this Merrick fellow" is. Merrick's first appearance in Teddie's room is more like a manifestation: "It was as if the figure had slowly materialized during the night and had now reached a stage of total conviction about itself and its surroundings" (T 113). Teddie finds him "ready" to be his best man; Barbie unexpectedly discovers Merrick alone at Rose Cottage; Perron arrives in Mirat and is amazed to find him married to Susan (Merrick's sudden intrusions in the narrative are similarly surprising for the reader—Merrick is never introduced, he always appears suddenly). His transformation into a wounded, scarred officer, who should be pitied, is of course another part of the invention. Sarah sums Merrick up when she thinks he is "a man obsessed by self-awareness" (S 339) because to be self-aware is not simply to be aware of oneself but of how one appears to others.

Finally, Merrick reaches his apogee in death. In his own scheme of things this is a glory-death that realizes the envy and fear felt towards him by others. Yet, in Scott's symbolic pattern it is necessary for Merrick to perish when the raj dies because he has attempted to create himself in its image; his death is also the nemesis of his presumption, hence Scott's use of the official story that Merrick has fallen, Satan-like, into the Nullah. Merrick achieves his own apotheosis in what is really the proof that he cannot escape his past.

In terms of identity, as I noted earlier, Hari is Merrick's Indian counterpart. Poised between the imposed stereotypes of English public schoolboy and faceless Indian under the raj, Hari is always trying, vainly, to find who he is. His only option is to reject both stock images. Merrick, however, considers himself from the same point of view from which he considers others—which is from the outside or stereotypically. Everyone has to perceive this reflected self—indeed it is only through a dialogical interraction that individuals can balance their view of themselves in the world, as with Barbie and the unknown Indian. However, Merrick reduces himself to this image, promoting the reflected, closed perception of himself far above the open, ever-present perception.

Hari and Merrick are equally victims of different prejudices, race and class respectively. Each defines his identity in terms of that discrimination. For Hari, a reconstruction is begun by his father and Hari is merely complicit with this "forgery" which to him is experientially "genuine." He is not aware of the importance and force of his difference until he arrives in India. From then on, Hari wishes to regain aspects of his past, until its distance from him lends it the unreal quality of a dream that he can dispel. For Merrick, the process is in many ways opposite. He has always been aware of his difference and wishes to reconstruct his identity by overwriting the palimpsest of his past.

Hari's story in the *Quartet* is one of disintegration through repeated exposures to prejudice and humiliation. Merrick's story is one of integration as he acquires the power and behaviour that will create a reflection in others that is superior, in his mind, to the one that is predicated on his passions, status, and social identity. He proposes for himself an alternative personality, equally stereotypical as Hari's, but one that, as it happens, no longer exists outside of his mind.

Social stereotyping along lines of class, which affects Hari and Merrick more than any other characters, is inevitable for Scott:

> You can't be English and alive without being sensitive to the class problem. . . . I don't think an English writer can write a novel without class being in the background, even if it's not consciously written in; class can't be detached from the English novel.[17]

The same could be said of the Indian novel, and the link introduced by Perron between Hari and the concepts of karma and dharma parallels Merrick's class-consciousness. Hari is a victim of "caste" as Merrick is of class.[18] It is common for these two hierarchies to be related:

> In many ways the social order of the raj resembled the caste system of the Hindus. At the top, corresponding to the priestly caste of the Brahmins, there were the senior government services. . . . Then there was the military order, corresponding to the Hindu warrior caste, the Kshatrias. . . . Next in the social order came the British businessmen, corresponding closely to the low-caste Vaisyas. . . . The fourth Hindu caste was that of the Sudras, the outcasts, which as far as Anglo-India was concerned meant the ordinary British soldier. . . .[19]

Despite their differences, their antagonism, and their achievements, Merrick and Hari are connected by the "importance" of class. Both suffer rejection and loneliness because of its pervasiveness. Hari falls from a position high on the class-ladder to its foot, while Merrick brings pain to himself and others by trying to climb up from one of its lower rungs. Hari falls because he is restricted by stereotypes of class and race, whereas Merrick climbs by using any means he can to tighten the artificial, stereotypical impression he produces on people. So Merrick is a man who, in Fenny Grace's words, has "made something of himself"

(S 407). If we ask what it is that Merrick has made, one answer is given by Daphne. Merrick's role as devil, for Barbie, is supplemented by an inverse of the "black devil" cliché through Daphne's theory of the "white robot" who is not a hot-tempered, wily, and impassioned tempter but a cold, programmed, and brutal official. This figure is clearly an updated model of Kipling's White Man.[20] Edward Said gives a thorough analysis of this figure and outlines its gross characteristics in terms reminiscent of Sartre's *engagement*:

> Behind the White Man's mask of amiable leadership there is always the express willingness to use force, to kill and be killed. What dignifies his mission is some sense of intellectual dedication; he is a White Man, but not for mere profit, since his "chosen star" presumably sits far above earthly gain. . . . One became a White Man because one *was* a White Man; more important, "drinking that cup," living that unalterable destiny in "the White Man's day," left one little time for idle speculation on origins, causes, historical logic.
>
> Being a White Man was therefore an idea and a reality. It involved a reasoned position towards both the white and nonwhite worlds. It meant—in the colonies—speaking in a certain way, behaving according to a code of regulations, and even feeling certain things and not others. It meant specific judgments, evaluations, gestures. It was a form of authority before which nonwhites, and even whites themselves, were expected to bend. . . . Being a White Man, in short, was a very concrete manner of being-in-the-world, a way of taking hold of reality, language, and thought.   (*Orientalism* 226-27)

Said might be describing Teddie's life and views here, but he also hints at Merrick's theories, at the conscious commitment to "taking hold of reality." The White Man in the *Quartet* is split between Teddie's embodiment of the "idea" and Merrick's *engagement* with the "reality"; one might say that Teddie is Merrick's mask, or that Merrick is the "willingness to use force" behind Teddie's "amiable leadership." Said identifies two historical factors in the construction of the White Man—and they apply to different halves of our split-subject. The first is inscribed in Merrick's theory of line-drawing: "the culturally sanctioned habit of deploying large generalizations by which reality is divided into various collectives: languages, races, types, colors, mentalities, each category being not so much a neutral designation as an evaluative interpretation. Underlying these categories is the rigidly binomial opposition of 'ours' and 'theirs'" (*Orientalism* 227). The second force applies to Teddie— who is far less rigid about enforcing the divisions between people and believes that a "nonwhite" person can "play the White Man" in a way that Merrick abhors.

However, the above discussion is limited to the notion of the White *Man*. For Daphne, Kipling's ideology has become so deeply ingrained that in the raj official, where questions of the White Man's unprejudiced and disinterested fairness must become matters of public concern, it is now "mechanical":

> even in my panic there was this assumption of superiority, of privilege, of believing I knew what was best for both of us, because the colour of my skin automatically put me on the side of those who never told a lie. But we've got far beyond that stage of colonial simplicity. We've created a blundering judicial robot. We can't stop it working. It works for us even when we least want it to. We created it to prove how fair, how civilised we are. But it is a white robot and it can't distinguish between love and rape. It only understands physical connexion and only understands it as a crime because it only exists to punish crime. (J 425)

Daphne's argument charts the corruption of the White Man's values as they become automatic and mechanical. Merrick is the epitome of Daphne's "White Robot," and in the next volume of the *Quartet* he will symbolize one by trading his natural arm for a prosthetic one and will continue to "invent" himself in the robot's image. It is also Daphne who identifies Merrick's self-denial and anticipates his destruction. In Bakhtin's terms she realizes that he has created himself in the mould of a stereotype and promoted a closed view of himself over an open one. In other words, she sees that his constructed self denies his personal one: "Whatever they felt that was original would die the moment it came into conflict with what the robot was geared to feel" (J 432). She also predicts what will happen when the robot learns to feel, when Merrick shows affection to those whom the robot despises: "One day someone may come along, cross a wire by mistake, or fix in a special circuit with the object of making it impartial and colour-blind, and then it will probably explode" (J 425). In Bronowsky's theory of Merrick's death-wish this is precisely what happens—Merrick recognizes his attraction to someone the robot would repulse, Aziz, and is killed. According to Bronowsky, a perceptive character who is the first to be aware of Merrick's homosexuality, Merrick is killed by his own beliefs. His death is therefore a sort of suicide or self-destruction. Bronowsky says Merrick suffered a "revelation of the connexion between the homosexuality, the sado-masochism, the sense of social inferiority and the grinding defensive belief in his racial superiority" (D 571). That is, Merrick is at war with himself—the image he has created is unable to exist with the human reality of loving an Indian boy.

132

CONCLUSION

Staying On at the Carnival

This carnival spirit offers the chance to have a new outlook on the world, to realize the relative nature of all that exists, and to enter a completely new order of things.   (Bakhtin, *RW* 34)

Paul Scott's last novel can be considered in relation to the *Quartet* as both a coda to and a parody of the tetralogy. *Staying On* deploys the subversive techniques and strategies associated with comedy in such a way as to suggest that their target is partly Scott's own work. In the context of Bakhtin's writings on carnival (a term he employs to represent those manifestations of a popular and democratic culture operating in opposition to a monologic and hierarchical official culture), I will suggest that *Staying On* works against the formality of the *Quartet* in order to mimic Scott's shift in subject from the British Empire to Indian Independence.

Staying On is sufficiently different from the *Quartet* that it almost seems like the work of another author. It is light, playful, inventive, and mocking; in fact, *Staying On* appears substantially to be a burlesque of the earlier novels, a defrocking of the solemnity of the *Quartet*, from whose periphery it steals its own major characters while relegating the principal Anglo-Indian character of the tetralogy, Sarah Layton, to the role of off-stage correspondent. It is a parody as Linda Hutcheon describes it: "a form of imitation but imitation characterized by ironic inversion, not always at the expense of the parodied text. . . . Parody is . . . repetition with critical distance, which marks differences rather than similarity" (5-6). But unlike most parodies, the original and the parodic derivative are in this case by the same writer. This is particularly relevant to an argument which considers *Staying On*'s life-affirming humour to be in the style of the satyr play, which Bakhtin notes was not simply a comedy but "originally the parodic and laughing aspect of the tragic trilogy that preceded it" (*PDP* 127). Just as the satyr plays were "parodic-travestying reworkings of national myth" (*DI* 55), Scott takes the myths of the raj and his own serious fiction, and leavens them both with ribaldry, bawdy, and farce. Of course, humour is also a way of obliquely attacking authority, and *Staying On* criticizes British Imperialism from an obtuse angle in comparison with the *Quartet*'s direct historical commentary. In Scott's final novel, the ideological authority of the Queen's English—and of officialdom, propriety, and ceremony—are undermined by the vulgar, the humorous, and the profane. The centralizing tendencies of centuries of British rule, under the proclaimed merits of a unifying judiciary, administration, and language, are placed in conflict with the licence of subaltern cultures, classes, and dialects.

Bakhtin's discussion of carnivalized literature in *Problems of Dostoevsky's Poetics* emphasizes that the ancient Greek world granted equal status to the serio-comical and the serious or "high" genres. The dominant features of this different and revolutionary form of literature were to become fundamental to the development of the novel. Bakhtin argues that the diverse texts that constitute the genre he terms "serio-comical" (into which *Staying On* falls) are bonded by the influence of carnival. The novels in this genre have three defining characteristics. First, they are concerned with the "living present" and "figures of the past are deliberately and emphatically contemporized" (*PDP* 108). From the 1947 of the *Quartet*'s close, both the Smalleys and, off-stage, the Laytons are moved twenty-five years forward to the context of India in the 1970s, when Scott was writing. The second feature, which Bakhtin considers inextricably tied up with the first, is that serio-comical works rely on experience and free-invention, not on "legend," and that they take a stance that "at times even resembles a cynical exposé" (*PDP* 108). For Scott, the shift away from a reliance on history, both contemporary with the end of the raj and prior to it (notably the massacre at Amritsar in 1919 and the conflict of 1857), is quite as important to the theme of independence as is the change to comic characters and satiric situations. Thirdly, there is the "deliberate multi-styled and hetero-voiced nature" of the serio-comical. The *Quartet* is remarkable for its historical sweep, for the numerous voices it orchestrates around relatively few incidents. Yet the accents and stresses of most of those voices are in many ways similar: European or Westernized, middle- or upper-class, intelligent and sincere, reflective and informed. *Staying On* is different again, because, in the style of carnival, it is socially inclusive and its pages are enriched by a wealth of human diversity. The carnival approach also imitates the greatly reduced sense of importance of those Britons who stayed on in India, who, relieved of the "burden" of government, feel themselves to be lighter also: "Mr. Bhoolabhoy had often heard it said that one of the troubles with the British in the days of the raj was that they had taken themselves far too seriously[;] . . . it was being responsible for running things that shortened the temper and destroyed the sense of humour" (117).

134

Having scratched the surface of their differences, I shall show in the remainder of this discussion how the post-colonial *Staying On* functions as carnivalized literature satirizing elements of the *Quartet*, parodying the serious treatment of the hierarchical structure in Scott's earlier fiction. It exemplifies Bakhtinian parody (as described at *DI* 51-54) in three key ways. First, *Staying On* consistently undercuts the serious tone of the tetralogy (Tusker's disrespectfulness, Lucy's play-acting, Ibrahim's excessive regard for the raj). Secondly, it uses the same location (Pankot), several of the same characters (the Layton family and the Smalleys—though they are reversed in terms of narrative foreground and background), and similar discourses (the raj and its beliefs are points of reference throughout the novel). Lastly, while admitting the above point, it is still true to say that *Staying On* in no way belongs to the genre of the previous four novels—a parody is always "of" a genre but never belongs to it.

After the *Quartet*, *Staying On* appears to contain an atmosphere in which, to use Bakhtin's words, "all *distance* between people is suspended, and a special carnival category goes into effect: *free and familiar contact among people*" (*PDP* 123). One of the novel's most memorable scenes focuses on the Holi spring fertility festival, where Tusker, the only surviving representative of the raj administration, plays the buffoon; to emphasize the point of this transformation, Scott has him powder-painted like a clown. Tusker is seen

> leaving the adults and joining the children, submitting first to their shyly thrown little handfuls of powder, then egging them on by shying back, so that presently they showered him with blue, purple and crimson powder and he returned to the adults covered from head to foot, his clothes caked, his eyes and teeth gleaming through the mask of coloured dust like a miner coming up from a pit where the devil's rainbow had its source. (174)

In this post-raj, or rather post-*Raj Quartet*, culture, where a retired British colonel plays wholeheartedly with Indian children, there are also what Bakhtin calls "*carnivalistic mésulliunces*" in which the characters, like the powders on Tusker's face, are mixed together, as "things that were once self-enclosed, disunified, distanced from one another by a noncarnivalistic hierarchical worldview are drawn into carnivalistic contacts and combinations" (*PDP* 123). In *Staying On*, the raj's hierarchy has faded, and though there are still servants and employers, bosses and subordinates, they are seen to interact. Also, as so rarely in the *Quartet*, members of different social groups talk freely to each other, and through this the book derives much of its humour (the social and cultural barriers that were deleteriously divisive in the earlier novels are here a source of farcical misunderstandings). Moreover, the pleasures of the body are foregrounded in *Staying On*. There is eating, excreting, dancing, singing, drinking and even ritual record-playing, all to an extent unequalled in the four long volumes of the *Quartet*. Most significantly, laughter, often sympathetic, extends to sex, illness, and death, and no area of the body or its functions remains taboo. (Bakhtin points out that folk humour led to "grotesque realism" in which "the bodily element is deeply positive. It is presented not in a private, egotistic form, severed from the other spheres of life, but as something universal, representing all the people" [*RW* 19].)

Two other notable elements of carnival are exemplified in Tusker Smalley and constitute his most prominent characteristics: eccentricity and profanation. The first brings out "the latent sides of human nature," while the second forms "a whole system of carnivalistic debasings and bringings down to earth, carnivalistic obscenities linked with the reproductive power of the earth and the body, carnivalistic parodies on sacred texts and sayings, etc." (*PDP* 123). An apposite example of *Staying On*'s puncturing of the seriousness of the earlier novels and of Tusker's ridiculing of the past is his studious rewriting of Edgar Maybrick's "A Short History of Pankot." Tusker's delight at one point focuses on Maybrick's observation that Mabel Layton was the last person to be buried in St. John's cemetery (100). Eager to rupture the inflated authority of Mr. Maybrick, Tusker is able to pronounce this a mistake, as Maybrick was himself the last person to be buried in the graveyard. This is important because in the *Quartet*, Mabel Layton's burial is a serious matter, embracing themes of guilt, purgatorial suffering, improper burial, and the haste with which the raj disposed of its responsibility in India. It leads Barbie Batchelor to madness, ostracism, and talk of disinterment. Its resurfacing in Tusker's childish quibbles is a way of moderating the "gravity" of the earlier work by treating death with less solemnity and less reverence. In *Staying On*, Mabel Layton's gravestone becomes simply a text to help Joseph, the *mali*, learn to read (150).

Almost everything that was repressed or clandestine in the *Quartet* is treated lightly in *Staying On*. Sex in the tetralogy is usually secretive and furtive, and brings to mind Ronald Merrick's sadism, Daphne Manners's rape, Sarah Layton's abortion, her mother's seemingly joyless adultery, and the scandal of Barbie Batchelor's rumoured "unnatural" love for Sarah and Susan. In *Staying On*, sex for Lucy means, on the one hand, charting the reality of Tusker's regularity in wanting intercourse (90) and, on the other, indulging in the fantasy of the batman Toole before

136

having a blue-rinse at the Seraglio room (198). For Mr. Bhoolabhoy, sex means the reality of his wife Lila's demands for coition, which depend on her success at bridge (9), and the fantasy of Hot Chicanya's exotic play-acting (119). In *Staying On*, the sex scenes are a celebration of the comic situations of everyday life that develop from a common animal urge, such as Mr. Bhoolabhoy's morning-after technique for extricating himself from under Lila without waking her (120) or Ibrahim's *coitus interruptus* with Edward Bingham's old ayah Minnie, who now works for Mrs. Bhoolabhoy (44). Sex is freed from its serious associations and turned into a source of fantasy, pleasure, and farce.

Even the religious guilt associated with sex is parodied in Mr. Bhoolabhoy's peccadilloes, intoned with the high solemnity of confession: "I am guilty of the sin of adultery with a lady in Ranpur and of the sin of lascivious expectation, item, the purchase of an unseemly garment for Koshak Dance, not having been content to call it a day with double-Lotus, but then chickening out and so committing the sin of failing to keep a promise" (145-46). In the *Quartet*, Christian communication with God is of an entirely different nature, not concerned with individual weaknesses but with the sins of a nation—most clearly where God's silence before Barbie Batchelor mimics a profound loss of faith in the raj's "mission" in India.

Bakhtin observes that the "primary carnivalistic act is the *mock crowning and subsequent decrowning of the carnival king*" (*PDP* 124). Irreverent and scatological, *Staying On* has its own coronation and deposits the last remaining members of the raj on their twin "thunder-boxes," their seats of empire. Tusker Smalley has his first heart-attack squatting on one of the "viceregal thrones" (44), and the novel ends with Lucy sitting like the Empress of India after the death of Albert: "She . . . glanced at the empty throne beside her, then shut her eyes. . . . 'I can't afford to cry. I have a performance to get through tomorrow. And another performance to get through on Wednesday. And on Thursday'" (255). This tragicomic treatment is emblematic of the raj's abdication and of its necessarily temporary rule:

> Crowning/decrowning is a dualistic ambivalent ritual, expressing the inevitability and at the same time the creative power of the shift-and-renewal, the *joyful relativity* of all structure and order, of all authority and all (hierarchical) position. Crowning already contains the idea of immanent decrowning: it is ambivalent from the very start. And he who is crowned is the antipode of a real king, a slave or a jester; this act, as it were, opens and sanctifies the inside-out world of carnival. (*PDP* 124)

137

In *Staying On,* Lucy and Tusker are the Viceroy and Vicereine of an inverted hierarchy, but they only take up their thrones together on one occasion, to perform the functions of a suitably Rabelaisian ceremony. It is when they both have diarrhoea: "halfway through the performance Tusker had begun to laugh and after a while she had begun to laugh too, so there they had been, enthroned, laughing like drains" (253). This is the most extreme description of a mixture of high and low; the enthroned raj of post-Independence India sit in state, laughing and excreting. Once more Scott evinces the comic side to a subject he had previously presented as anything but comic—in the *Quartet,* the incidence of dysentery among the British in India was a serious issue, reducing Teddie Bingham's life to misery, humbling Robin White, and prompting Leonard Purvis' suicide.

That life under the raj was one big performance, its members always on show and "representing something," is parodied in Lucy Smalley's penchant for consciously acting out situations. Her performances are greatly admired by the pro-raj Ibrahim: "Himself an old devotee of Hollywood films, as she was, [Ibrahim] knew Memsahib was about to go into her Bette Davis bit" (35). Ibrahim shares Lucy's passion for certain movies and her fantasies of dramatic heroines who are every bit as convincing in the roles they play as the memsahibs were in theirs. Lucy's desire to be an actress mimics her desire now to be an avatar of the pukka mems—confident, composed, and almost regal, but also ready for romance and adventure. One such fantasy is reminiscent of the opening image of the *Quartet*: "She could be anything and anyone she wished. Within the darkness of her closed eyes and enfolding palms she was suddenly—how strange—Renée Adorée running after the truck taking Jack Gilbert away to the front in *The Big Parade*" (198).

On a thematic level, Ibrahim is interested in old Hollywood films because he is nostalgic about the histrionics of the raj. For him, Tusker and Lucy inevitably embody the roles which were, ironically, denied them in the *Quartet,* so that when Lucy underpays the *mali* by one rupee it merely confirms "his opinion of her as a lady of style" (73), and when she reacts calmly to news of Tusker's worsening condition, Ibrahim observes: "True memsahibs never panicked" (32). When Ibrahim thinks of movie stars, they are the noble heroines of "women's" pictures from the late thirties, before the end of the raj. He is drawn to strong-willed, suffering Western women who "never panicked": "he had seen at last how Greta Garbo died at the end of *Camille,* how Bette Davis died at the end of *Dark Victory* and sat desolate on a chair in the Tower at the end of *Elizabeth and Essex* [*sic*]. In a London cinema he had watched Vivien

138

Leigh running through the mist at the end of *Gone With the Wind*" (72). And it is no coincidence that Lucy is left at the end of Scott's novel sitting, like Bette Davis in Ibrahim's memories, "desolate on a chair." Scott's last novel is parodic partly because it allies the raj with contemporaneous Hollywood productions, and yet it creates further mockery in the reader's mind through Ibrahim's sentimental indulgence in the movies, which is associated with his reverential attitude towards the raj.

Another aspect of the carnivalized text significant to *Staying On* is its location. Carnivalization calls for a place (such as the film-theatre, for example) which provides "meeting and contact-points for heterogeneous people" (*PDP* 128). The public square is the traditional place for carnival and indeed this is where Tusker, across the enormous gulf of generations and experience, meets the only other Englishman in Pankot, a young Liverpudlian hippie who is as representative of supposedly "degenerate" culture in Britain as Tusker is representative of the decayed raj in India. (Begging his food from Ibrahim, the hippie metonymically represents the West's attempts to learn from what it perceives to be the ascetic spiritualism of the East as much as Mrs. Bhoolabhoy's capitalism signifies an attempt to gain from the ways of the West.) But Scott's chief public space is that of the hotels, Smith's and the Shiraz, where staff and public, business people and celebrities, tourists and locals, long-term residents and overseas visitors, "management and ownership," all mix together in the traditional melting-pot of carnival life. Bakhtin notes that in the European social-adventure novels of the nineteenth century the most essential feature "is an application of carnivalization to the portrayal of contemporary reality and contemporary everyday life; *everyday life* is drawn into the carnivalized action of the plot; the ordinary and constant is combined with the extraordinary and changeable" (*PDP* 158). In its emphasis on the contemporary and the confluence of the ordinary and extraordinary in everyday life (for example, Mr. Bhoolabhoy is equally a friend to Colonel Smalley, a Church of England lay-preacher, a sex-show aficionado, and an hotel manager), *Staying On* differs from the earlier *Quartet* as much as it does in its stress on comedy.

Importantly, Scott's last novel is also full of misunderstandings and manipulations, mostly built around the deception of Tusker and Lila over "Operation *Mali*." The aggregate of intrigue in ordinary lives is summed up by Lucy, quoting the words of another Scott, from *Marmion*: "Oh what a tangled web we weave, once we practise to deceive. Even for the best of reasons and for but a limited time" (48). Lucy is referring to the deception over who has employed the *mali*, but the quotation encompasses the entire narrative: Mr. Bhoolabhoy adulterously deceives Mrs. Bhoolabhoy, Lila (quite legally) deceives the Smalleys over their contract, Lucy deceives Tusker over Mr. Turner's visit, and Ibrahim deceives Lucy over the *mali*'s pay. Scott uses the machinations at the heart of the carnival plot, mistake and deception, to create pathos and farce around the central premise of an enclave of the raj still billeted in modern India: temporally, the Smalleys are the last, ridiculous "outpost of empire."

Thus the novel has themes of deception and also of ignorance, and the comedy of Ibrahim's relationships with Joseph and Tusker is founded on the roles of bogus learned teacher and unworldly pupil. Without the additional use of deception, the novel weaves confusion around the basic activity of trying to comprehend what others say. For Bakhtin, this is fundamental to the carnival plot:

> Stupidity (incomprehension) in the novel is always polemical: it interacts dialogically with an intelligence (a lofty pseudo intelligence) with which it polemicizes and whose mask it tears away . . . [A]t its heart always lies a polemical failure to understand someone else's discourse, someone else's pathos-changed lie that has appropriated the world and aspires to conceptualize it, a polemical failure to understand generally accepted, canonized, inveterately false languages with their lofty labels for things and events.

> (*DI* 403)

In its simplest form, incomprehension features whenever Joseph is incapable of understanding Ibrahim, not least because of Ibrahim's misplaced but unwavering confidence in his rightness (an appropriate reminder of the self-belief of the raj in which Ibrahim also had faith). However, it is chiefly the reader who comprehends the irony of, for example, Ibrahim's reverence for Tusker's profanity, as when he explains "bugger-off" in terms of a holy proverb or wise saying: "It is a very old English phrase meaning *jeldi jao*. Likewise piss-off. These are sacred phrases, Joseph" (64). Tusker's constant profanity is typical of carnival familiarity, which Bakhtin outlines thus: "It is characteristic for the familiar speech of the marketplace to use abusive language, insulting words or expressions, some of them quite lengthy and complex. The abuse is grammatically and semantically isolated from context, and regarded as something of a proverb" (*RW* 16). Abusive language is seen as positively healthy and so, when Tusker asserts he will sue Lila "from arsehole to Christmas," its only significance for Ibrahim is "Sahib was on the mend" (29).

These disparate characters, Ibrahim, Tusker, and Joseph, can be seen to perform three of the key roles of carnival, in relation to language and the undermining of authority: the rogue, the clown, and the fool. Bakhtin writes:

> [T]he rogue's gay deception parodies high languages, the clown's malicious distortion of them, his turning them inside out and finally the fool's naive incomprehension of them—these three dialogic categories that had organized heteroglossia in the novel at the dawn of its history emerge in modern times with extraordinary surface clarity and are embodied in the symbolic images of the rogue, the clown and the fool. (*DI* 405)

These can be taken as outlines for the three males of the Smalley household. First, Ibrahim, as likable rogue, is always looking out for number one, but is never malicious. He is constantly wheeling and dealing in the smallest markets: playing the Smalleys off against each other, making money from Lucy and from the *mali*, getting in free at the cinema, swigging the gin that Lucy soaks her rings in (32), and generally exercising his right to "discreetly appropriated perks" (30). His deception of Lucy and Joseph over the latter's pay is scheming, but Ibrahim simply sees himself as taking the intermediary's cut. He also serves as a conduit down which runs the "official" English language from Lucy and Tusker to the *mali*, and Ibrahim's confidence despite his mistakes provides much of the novel's humour. However, because of his wider experience, moving between social strata, Ibrahim has different expectations of the world from the Smalleys; this is brought out when Lucy innocently tells him that she wants a boy and he infers that she wants him to procure a male prostitute (40). Misunderstandings are profuse in the novel whenever members of different cultural groups try to communicate, and Ibrahim's petty deceptions simply take this semantic confusion into a physical arena.

Secondly, Tusker is the clown who entertains at parties, who speaks his own comic language, who always has his own individual sense of reality (as with his half-stubborn, half-paranoid refusal to acknowledge the *mali*). He has altered from the serious days of the *Quartet* to suit his new status under the Pankot *swaraj*:

> In the days before his personality change he'd had little sense of humour himself. . . . It had developed subsequently, but in almost knockabout pantomimic form. . . . There he was, in the garden of the oldest and most beautiful bungalow in Pankot, a gesticulating clown, coloured from head to foot and giving a performance that was not so much attracting attention as

forcing laughter from the immaculately dressed and well-behaved Indians whom he was haranguing, or telling some unseemly story to. (174-75)

This is a changed Tusker from the one who was deeply shocked by a psychiatrist saying the word "orgasm" to the Pankot memsahibs in *The Towers of Silence*. Tusker's "proper" position as epigone of the glorious and respectable raj is thus undermined, and the airs and graces of the departed rulers are most evident in the Indians of modern Pankot, just as the ambitions and distinctions of the raj are now shown in Mrs. Bhollabhoy's dreams of an empire of hotels, of "putting up concrete just like in the West" (193), and her strict division between private life (husband and wife) and business ("management and ownership"). While Tusker plays the clown, his hosts, Coocoo and Colonel "Tiny" Menektara, have come to live, as the Smalleys once did, in Mabel Layton's beautiful Rose Cottage. Tusker's antics represent an overturned world because, for Scott, the status of the raj's representatives in India has been inverted. While Tusker and Lucy have no authority in Pankot, Scott seems to suggest that the social standing of the raj, and to an extent its values, have been assumed by elements of middle-class India, and this comes out in his portrayals of Indian snobbery (for example, the prime minister of Pakistan is dismissed as "only a grocer's son" [176]). Lucy notices this reversal of positions in attitudes towards Tusker's dual roles in Pankot of dethroned ruler and clown: "it was obvious to Lucy that Coocoo was thinking: 'Yes, you're nice, you can be fun, you make us laugh, you're always welcome, but you're an Englishman so you represent the defeated enemy'" (173).

Then, thirdly, there is Joseph the *mali*, the fool of whom Bakhtin says: "by his very uncomprehending presence he makes strange the world of social conventionality" (*DI* 404). The *mali* is the innocent outsider who stands at the mouth of the ordinary garden shed "as though it were a holy grotto" (59) and has to be indoctrinated by the others into the ways of their society (though in Tusker's case it is only indirectly, through Ibrahim). His different understanding brings out affection in the main characters and their desire to educate. So, presumably ignorant of the truth, Ibrahim is touched by the *mali*'s belief that grass breathes (61), and Lucy is affected by his anxiety that God will confuse people's souls if Joseph mispronounces their names (149). After each of these incidents, the "simple boy," as Mr. Bhoolabhoy calls him (150), is taught by Ibrahim and Lucy in turn: several pages of the novel are spent on Ibrahim's explaining "all he felt it necessary for the young *mali* to know" (62-67), and the attempt at Joseph's induction in reading English is started by Lucy (150). The *mali* is in one sense the fool whose difference is marked by his unworldly qualities. However, he is also the "fool" who in fact possesses the qualities lacked by those for whom he is a fool: he is not interested in appropriating money (unlike Ibrahim, who thinks Joseph is therefore "not smart"), but works hard, enjoys caring for his environment, and prays sincerely.

Scott aims the idiosyncracies of each of these three characters at the raj and the solemnity of the *Quartet*. Ibrahim's self-promotion ridicules the values of the raj, Colonel Smalley's clowning mocks it, and the *mali*'s innocent incomprehension of their attitudes and their claims to knowledge reveals not his but their foolishness.

Scott's final novel suggests a period of transition in his reconstruction of the end and aftermath of the raj's influence in India, as some of its last representatives fade away and their demise is symbolized by the fate of Smith's hotel, shrunken beside the Shiraz. Since Independence, the fortunes of the small hotel have moved with the fluctuations in Pankot's popularity, but they now seem to be drowning in a tide of progress: "This had been the pattern since the days of the *raj*. After the *raj* went there had been bad times, good times, near-disastrous times, times of retrenchment, times of ebullient hope, as Pankot waxed, waned, waxed again in popularity. But for Smith's now it all seemed to be coming to an end" (12). Even the world of the movies has changed from the Hollywood studios and stars of Lucy's memory to the Indian companies who fly into Pankot and book a whole floor of the Shiraz. Most poignantly, the Smalleys are like Smith's beside the towering Shiraz: small, insignificant, expendable, looked-down-upon by the pukka elite:

> Watching them, Lucy realized that nothing had changed for *her*, because there was this new race of sahibs and memsahibs of international status and connection who had taken the place of generals and Mrs. Generals, and she and Tusker had become for them almost as far down in the social scale as the Eurasians were in the days of the *raj*. (214-15)

This last comment links Lucy with Susy Williams, the Eurasian woman she is going to ask to dinner but has never before shown any hospitality to, despite the fact that Susy "was now virtually their oldest acquaintance in Pankot" (204). Susy's exclusion is finally brought home as Lucy realises how she herself has always been, and still is, subject to the snobbery of others.

Scott's final novel is in dialogue with the *Quartet* and deliberately reveals and revels in the comic sides to life which the earlier novels play down in order to concentrate on issues of responsibility, prejudice, and injustice during the dismantling of a discredited imperial apparatus. In *Staying On* these themes are still present but are placed in the context of the other concerns which permeate the characters' lives. And the grand issues are themselves partly belittled by the minor forms they take: the end of the raj and Indian Independence are transposed into the manipulation of a hotel empire and the eviction of old tenants—the whole wrapped up in sexual disappointments, obscene jokes, petty deceptions, private fantasies, pedagogic persiflage, and comic misunderstandings. Because it is a novel that parodies the raj, Scott centres it on a couple who were in the margins of Anglo-India and yet who, comically, now occupy it wholly because they are its last misplaced, exiled, expiring, and finally homeless examples.

Staying On echoes the *Quartet* in myriad ways: the image of the girl running recurs in Lucy's fantasies of screen heroines; the importance of gardens is continued in the *mali*'s story; the theme of exiled prisoners equally describes the Smalley's predicament; and the departure and demise of the raj is given a final twist in Tusker's death and his abandonment of Lucy. In many ways, the title of Scott's final novel refers to his own inability to let the raj and the *Quartet* go. What he was able to relinquish was the tetralogy's form and tone, presenting the reader not with a fifth novel of portentous "tragedy" but a serio-comic carnivalesque masterpiece full of affectionate parody. In his book *Postmodernist Fiction*, Brian McHale points out the connections between Bakhtin's ideas and experimental contemporary novels: "postmodernist fiction has reconstituted both the formal and the topical or motival repertoires of carnivalized literature. In fact, it has gone even further than that in recovering its carnival roots" (173-74). Arguably, each of the carnival elements that McHale identifies in postmodernist writing is also found in *Staying On*: the "reduced version" of carnival in the brief scene at the Holi festival, the "parodies of official ceremonies" and "mock-coronation and dethronement," the emphases on sex, defecation, food, drink, blasphemy and profanity. It is a novel charged with pathos but one which refuses, in retrospect, to take the raj or the values of Anglo-India seriously. Above all, however, it refuses to take the *Quartet* seriously.

Staying On is thus one form of comment on the *Quartet*. Looking further afield, Scott's tetralogy has been variously received by Goonetilleke as a "major achievement," by Bergonzi as "distinguished," by Anthony Burgess as an anachronistic Victorian "shapeless monster," and by Storm Jameson as a work which would have been recognised and hailed as a classic had it been published fifty years earlier.[1] The one aspect that has been accorded general applause is the historical detail, from Zulfikar Ghose's tribute that "no one has recorded every aspect of the raj as brilliantly accurately as Mr. Scott" to R. K. Narayan's encomium that Scott's "descriptions display a remarkable understanding —more accurate than any British writer on Indian themes."[2] These comments reflect the fact that the *Quartet* is a deeply serious work concerned with exploring the effect of losing an empire on an insular island-people, its pre-eminent aim being to expose the roots and consequences of a racism ingrained in the British-Indian experience. Scott's immediate anxiety was for Britain in the sixties and seventies, where he could hear, in Enoch Powell's speeches and in defences of immigration laws, echoes of the prejudice of the raj. The *Quartet* and its complex use of images are therefore most helpfully seen as an examination of Scott's central concerns: division and racism, their basis in history, the consequences of exile, and the psychological condition of marginality.

NOTES

INTRODUCTION

1 *The Raj Quartet* consists of the following four novels: *The Jewel in the Crown, The Day of the Scorpion, The Towers of Silence,* and *A Division of the Spoils.* Hereafter it will be called simply the *Quartet.* In references throughout the text these novels will be cited as J, S, T, and D respectively.

2 Said, Introduction to Kipling's *Kim,* 11; Mahood, 208; Walsh, 177.

3 Copley, 58; Tarzie Vittachi, *The Brown Sahib (Revisited)* (Delhi: Penguin, 1987) 143, quoted by Gooneratne in Acheson 48.

4 For example, see the essays in *My Appointment with the Muse,* particularly "Enoch Sahib: A Slight Case of Cultural Shock," 91-104. Future references to *My Appointment with the Muse* throughout the text will be cited as M.

5 *Chronicle of the Twentieth Century,* 979. This rhetoric is still in evidence in the nineties. Many commentators likened a speech in May 1993 by a Conservative MP, Winston Churchill, to Powell's "rivers of blood" speech. Churchill claimed that the "British way of life" was being swamped by "immigrants" (*Times,* 29 May 1993: 1).

6 *Chronicle of the Twentieth Century,* 1008.

7 Imperialism was never acceptable to liberalism, which always held that it was wrong to restrict people's freedom, and that to use force to do so was doubly wrong. However, liberals could countenance and even believe in the Empire for reasons outlined by Carthill in 1924: "Liberalism insisted that this unlawful power, if retained, should be exercised for the good of the subject races. . . . [A]n Empire to endure must be founded on justice and mercy . . . [and] it is necessary that an Imperial race should feel that the possession and rule of empire is not merely a privilege but a burden" (Carthill, 124-25). The crisis for liberals came when the idea of a beneficent Empire was no longer tenable for them. Then, the liberal argument for the Empire changed increasingly into the liberal dilemma as liberals felt that power was not influenced "for the good of subject races."

8 *Times,* 6 January 1966: 15.

9 Scott, "India: A Post-Forsterian View" (Tulsa: II: 7: 10: 26).

10 Eagleton, 199-200. A comprehensive introduction to the history of liberal humanism is provided by Coates and White in *The Ordeal of Liberal Humanism.* The epilogue is particularly useful as it posits a revival of liberal humanism in the 1950s and 60s when Scott was writing (455), though, concerning itself with the vanquishing of extremist ideologies in Europe, it has little to say on racism, even anti-Semitism. Turning more particularly to literature, in the glossary to their book *Feminist Readings: Feminist Reading* Sara Mills et al. give the following definition of the liberal humanist critical stance: "a 'common sense' position where 'man' and his experience are at the centre of interest. Literary texts can be shown to have universal significance, speaking for all time of an unchanging transcendental human nature. The human mind is considered outside social relations and historical change" (244).

[11] Scott, draft review (Tulsa: III: 5: 65) of John Rosselli, *Lord William Bentinck: The Making of a Liberal Imperialist 1774-1839* (Berkeley: University of California Press), 1974. Eric Stokes's *The English Utilitarians in India* (Oxford: Oxford UP, 1959) is essential reading in this area.

[12] Scott, "India: A Post-Forsterian View" (Tulsa: II: 7: 10: 17).

[13] For a discussion of the influences of "Powellism," see Michael and Ann Dummett, "The Role of Government in Britain's Racial Crisis," especially 138-40.

[14] Scott, from one 1972 version of an essay entitled "The Form and Function of the Novel" (Tulsa: II: 8: 22: 6); Fowles's essay is "Notes Towards An Unfinished Novel," in *The Novel Today*, ed. Malcolm Bradbury 136-50.

[15] Like Scott and Fowles, Faulkner once spoke of this kind of image initiating a novel: "It began with a mental picture. I didn't realize at the time that it was symbolical. The picture was of the muddy seat of a little girl's drawers in a pear tree where she could see through a window where her grandmother's funeral was taking place . . ." (Interview with Jean Stein vanden Heuvel, included in *The Sound and the Fury*, Norton Critical Edition [1987] 240).

[16] Scott, who refused to call himself a historical novelist because he had lived through the events he chronicled, was all the same deeply concerned with the pressure of the times and the importance of what he called the "drift of history," a movement of events and moral beliefs acting on the conscience and the actions of an age.

[17] The word "race" is accorded quotation marks here, but not in later chapters, to signal the issues associated with the term (i.e. "race" is meaningless in terms of human biology, but there is still "racism")—see Todorov " 'Race,' Writing, and Culture" in Gates, 370-71.

[18] Miss Crane, even though her liberal instincts do not stretch far enough, embodies Scott's own beliefs in this respect: "She had devoted her life, in a practical and unimportant way, trying to prove that fear was evil because it promoted prejudice . . . that ignorance was bad because fear sprang from it" (J 21).

[19] Benedict Anderson writes that colonial racism generalized "a principle of innate, inherited superiority on which its own domestic position was (however shakily) based to the vastness of the overseas possessions, covertly (or not so covertly) conveying the idea that if, say, English lords were naturally superior to other Englishmen, no matter: these other Englishmen were no less superior to the subjected natives" (*Imagined Communities* 150).

[20] The embrace is portrayed from an Indian perspective in Gita Mehta's novel, *Raj*: "Everywhere in India the people are linking arms. One day the Empire will wake up and find itself strangled in our embrace" (67).

[21] Scott's opinion of English responsibility for the history of India after Independence is exactly summed up in the circumstances of Ahmed's death. The British thought "that he would be quite safe so long as he went of his own free will. But all the evidence suggests that the witness was right about the words and the expression. The victim chose neither the time nor the place" (D 113).

[22] However, as we will see later, the choice of any causal starting-point is problematic, and the events of August 1942 are themselves presaged by much that went before, not only in history, but also in the *Quartet*'s extension into its own fictional past.

[23] See Schwarz (1992) and Colwell (1996).

CHAPTER ONE

[1] See, for example, his essay entitled "After Marabar: Britain and India, A Post-Forsterian View" in *My Appointment with the Muse.*

[2] Commented on, for example, by Oliver Stallybrass in his introduction to *A Passage to India,* 8.

[3] For Forster's reaction, see Stallybrass's introduction to *A Passage to India,* 12.

[4] According to Sara Suleri: "To the imperial English mind, India can only be represented as a gesture of possible rape" (246), while Brenda Silver argues that in both Dr. Aziz's and Hari's case "the Indian man, reduced to his sexuality, becomes simultaneously rapist and object of rape" (Silver, 94). A simple expression of this in fiction comes in Orwell's *Burmese Days*: "To [Mrs. Lackersteen's] mind the words "sedition," "National-ism," "rebellion," "Home Rule," conveyed one thing and one only, and that was a picture of herself being raped by a procession of jet-black coolies with rolling white eyeballs" (156).

[5] Also worthy of note is Forster's portrayal of Adela (accusing, manipulated, silent) compared with Scott's portrayal of Daphne (unaccusing, resistant to social pressure, and, though silent to the world, confessional to her diary).

[6] This is insightfully discussed from both Eastern and Western standpoints in Gita Mehta's book *Karma Cola.*

[7] N. C. Chaudhuri's essay is reprinted in Rutherford (68-78).

[8] "Freud, like Bakhtin . . . sees the self as divided; it 'is fallen apart into two pieces, one of which rages against the second . . . the piece which behaves so cruelly is not unknown to us . . . We have called it the "ego ideal," and by way of functions we have ascribed to it self-observation, the moral conscience, the censorship of dreams, and the chief influ-ence in repression.'" Holquist, 1990, 53, quoting Bakhtin.

[9] See also C 241, 293 and M 137.

[10] Scott, review of Ved Mehta's *Portrait of India* (Tulsa: III: 4: 39).

[11] Suleri, 245. The same can be and has been said of *Heart of Darkness*: "Conrad is concerned not so much with Africa as with the deterioration of one European mind" (Achebe 8). Conrad *uses* Africa for this end; Scott's decline of the raj is, by contrast, set in India by necessity.

[12] Evelyn Baring Cromer, quoted in Said, *Orientalism* 36.

[13] Said notes that in *Daniel Deronda* the Orient "has plans made for it," but another example would be Harold Transome in *Felix Holt* about whom F. C. Thomson notes in his introduction to the Oxford edition (1988): "'I'm an Oriental, you know,' says Harold, and the term carries here overtones of a nomadic, alien character, lacking a sense of English traditions and institutions" (xvi).

[14] Quoted in Stallybrass's introduction to *A Passage to India,* 23.

[15] Forster in appendix III to *A Passage to India* (1985) 307.

[16] Sir Alfred Lyall quoted in Said, *Orientalism* 38.

CHAPTER TWO

[1] Patrick Swinden has even argued that Scott's novels could be said *to be about* the loss of paradise (1).

[2] Emma Roberts, an early nineteenth-century traveller in India, quoted in Palling, 233.

³ The most thorough and insightful discussion of women in Scott's tetralogy is the chapter on the *Quartet* entitled "The Ruins of Time" in Sharpe.

⁴ *The Towers of Silence*: Austin: 6: insert page "t."

⁵ "Corrected TMS for TV Book Programme" (Tulsa: 2: 11: 19).

⁶ Walker writes with respect to the equation of paradise and garden in the world's mythologies: "The Persian Pairidaeza (Paradise) was a magic garden surrounding the holy mountain of the gods, where the Tree of Life bore the fruit of immortality. Pairidaeza was also the divine Virgin. . . . Hebrew *pardes*, 'garden,' was derived from the same Virgin paradise" (768).

⁷ The aspects of violence and protection (Mr. Chaudhuri's attempt to protect Miss Crane, Daphne's attempt to protect Hari) that are present in Daphne's and Miss Crane's ordeals, echo the past: "There is blood on her torn bodice. Her name is Janet MacGregor. A Muslim servant called Akbar Hossain died defending her" (J 64). These are partly variations on the story of Miss Sherwood at Amritsar, protected from her attackers by an Indian household (discussed in chapter 4).

⁸ This element of recurrence, involving the past with the present, was stronger in Scott's early conceptions of *The Jewel in the Crown*. One plan included the device of a Western film crew in India shooting the story of Daphne Manners and the Bibighar in the 1960s — thus broadening out the third temporal plane of the future (which has been pared down to the thoughts of the narrator in the published novel).

⁹ Margaret Scanlan terms Rose Cottage the "Eden of Anglo-India" (144).

¹⁰ For mention of Eden in the Koran see the chapter called "The Creator" (181). The importance of the garden (and of fire) to Kasim is the same as it is for the members of the raj: e.g. "Those that have faith and do good works shall be received in the gardens of Paradise, as a reward for that which they have done. But those that do evil shall be cast into the Fire"—chapter entitled "Adoration," 188.

¹¹ This event is actually prepared for at the start of *The Day of the Scorpion*: "Some of those that remain still mourn friends and relatives who chose Islam but never reached that land of promise, having died on the way, some of illness, many by violence. Sometimes a train they travelled on would pass one coming out of Islam. . . . These people mourned too for what they had left behind and for friends and relatives who started on the journey with them but did not live to finish it" (S 2).

¹² Lady Chatterjee suggests that all of India is a "repository" for the raj: "You all went, but left so much behind that you couldn't carry with you wherever you were going . . ." (J 451).

¹³ With respect to Miss Crane's words "too late," subsequently taken up by Barbie, Scott writes the following in the draft of an essay he wrote for *John Kenneth Galbraith Introduces India*: "About the raj now there descended a certain melancholy of a people who had to face a stiffening opposition in the country of their voluntary exile and the more disagreeable opposition which came from home. Feeling itself unloved, the declining years of the raj were, I believe, years in which the remote affection always implicit in paternalism became a different, deeper emotion. Too late" ("The Raj" [Tulsa: II: 9: 15: 27]).

¹⁴ *The Towers of Silence*: Austin: 6: 105.

¹⁵ *The Jewel in the Crown*: Austin: 1: no page number. The passage is from the *Young Kumar* section (the character speaking here is Mr. Francis Narayan, who appears in "Miss Crane" [e.g. J 27]).

16 Scott, version of "India: A Post-Forsterian View" (Tulsa: II: 7: 10: 30).

17 Scott wrote: "I do think . . . that it is probably important to remember how cut off the imperialist British became from the general movement of their own Society at home. Their final position was that of stranded whales, or minnows. I try to illustrate something of that in the Scorpion book, particularly in poor Sarah" (Scott quoted in Moore, 87).

18 The entrenched insularity of the British abroad is of course a common observation, as in this example from Scott's favourite nineteenth-century novelist, Thackeray: "Those who know the English colonies abroad know that we carry with us our pride, pills, prejudices, Harvey-sauces, cayenne-peppers, and other Lares, making a little Britain wherever we settle down" (*Vanity Fair*, chapter 64). By contrast, Orwell is scathing of the Anglo-Indians who return to Britain and maintain their exile: "Do you know these Anglo-Indian families? It's almost impossible when you get inside these people's houses, to remember that out in the street it's England and the twentieth century. As soon as you set foot inside the front door you're in India in the eighties. You know the kind of atmosphere. The carved teak furniture, the brass trays, the dusty tiger-skulls on the wall, the Trichinopoly cigars, the red-hot pickles, the yellow photographs of chaps in sun-helmets, the Hindustani words that you're expected to know the meaning of, the everlasting anecdotes about tiger-shoots and what Smith said to Jones in Poona in '87. It's a sort of little world of their own that they've created, like a kind of cyst" (*Coming Up for Air*, chapter 10).

CHAPTER THREE

1 Projected opening to *The Towers of Silence*: Austin: 6: 18.

2 Scott would very regretfully have agreed with the following statement by H. V. Hodson written in the year after Independence: "the feeling among the British public is relief at the laying down of a burden, mingled with thankfulness that Britain does not have to take responsibility for the ghastly troubles that have overtaken parts of the Indian subcontinent since authority was handed over" (Hodson, 102).

3 Cf. Coleridge, Chapter XVII of *Biographia Literaria*: "For *facts* are valuable to a wise man, chiefly as they lead to the discovery of the indwelling *law*, which is the true *being* of things."

4 Scott wrote, in a draft of *The Towers of Silence*: "Barbie, on August 6, with her shadow on the wall, as if burnt into it by the heat of an unimaginable flame. The shadow on the wall proclaimed the death of the age of anxiety and the beginning of the age of certainty of our destruction" (note attached to end of *The Towers of Silence*: Austin: 6). The shadow is also linked with one cause of Barbie's death, her trunk of mission property and relics which, we will see, is an image of the raj's burden of history: "[it] was merely luggage she knew, but without it she did not seem to have a shadow" (T 8-9).

5 Emerson, "Love," 202.

6 The original title of *The Towers of Silence*, "The Apotheosis of Barbara Batchelor," suggests the line in the passage above from Emerson's essay: "love, which is the deification of persons." Barbie's life in *The Towers of Silence* can be summarized as a movement towards the realization of the failure of her love for others and her repentance of this fact. Barbie "long[s] for an apotheosis" as a reward for her "love" (see T 65).

[7] All linkages in the novels are not only examples of "going in through the back of the image," but also illustrations of Emerson's view that we can see explanations of our own lives in those of others and vice versa.

[8] Emerson, "History", 109-10.

[9] "The White Man's Burden," *The Definitive Edition of Rudyard Kipling's Verse*, 323.

[10] One critic's description of Emerson's essay structure, organized around a central idea, is also well suited to convey how Scott shaped *The Jewel in the Crown*, and then the tetralogy, from a generating image: "in an ascending and widening spiral around a fixed center, which is the major idea" (D. F. Finnigan quoted in Scheick, x). In the *Quartet*, history is always shown to be a variation on the circumstances of the Bibighar: the past contains situations which seem to derive a particular meaning from their relation to this central major event. The clearest description of this is given by Sir George Malcolm: "[people] sometimes found the solution to the problem they were evading by going round in ever *increasing* circles and disappearing into the centre of *those*, which, relatively speaking, coincided with the centre of the circle from whose periphery they had evasively spiralled outwards" (D 318). Cf. Emerson: "The life of man is a self-evolving circle, which, from a ring imperceptibly small, rushes on all sides outwards to new and larger circles, and that without End" (quoted by Sherman Paul in Konvitz and Whicher, 176).

[11] Lawrence, quoted in Bradbury and McFarlane, *Modernism*, 51.

[12] *New Science*, par. 1108.

[13] Said, "On Repetition," *The World, the Text, and the Critic*, 113.

[14] *Oxford Companion to the Mind*, 318.

[15] At one stage Scott had an intention for a different sequel to *The Jewel in the Crown*, which was to contain a literal re-enactment of the Bibighar: "as it is seen historically [with a] repetition of earlier dramatic circumstances, e.g. a replay against the background of changed circumstances" (quoted in Moore, 73).

CHAPTER FOUR

[1] Aristotle, *Poetics*, 17, and Hayden White, "The Historical Text as Literary Artifact," 42.

[2] Reece, introduction to *My Appointment with the Muse*, 5.

[3] Butterfield, in the preface to *The Whig Interpretation of History*, speaks of "the tendency in many historians to write on the side of Protestants and Whigs, to praise revolutions provided they have been successful, to emphasize certain principles of progress in the past and to produce a story which is the ratification if not the glorification of the present." This is exactly Scott's point about liberal histories and unrecorded men. Butterfield also thinks all history has a tendency to "veer over into whig history," especially as it becomes more selective or abridged (6-7). In addition, Butterfield follows Emerson and anticipates Scott in writing that the "primary assumption of all attempts to understand the men of the past must be the belief that we can in some degree enter into minds that are unlike our own. . . . In reality the historian postulates that the world is in some sense always the same world" (9).

[4] This relation is something Scott tries to argue for by writing with what Bernard Bergonzi (who, curiously, reserves this quality for what he terms "historical fiction proper") calls "a sense of the interpenetration of past and present, and of the extent to which our own collective past still affects us" (225).

5 Tariq Ali is the critic who has most clearly recognized Scott's intention here, commenting that his novels lead to the conclusion that: "racism in contemporary Britain is closely related to the colonial experience" ("Fiction as History, History as Fiction").

6 Interestingly, while the "Mutiny" (as it has been known to the British—Indian views are better represented in the title of V. D. Savarkar's book, *The Indian War of Independence of 1857*) features prominently in dozens of works of English fiction on India, from Sir George Trevelyan's *Cawnpore* (1865), through the novels of Flora Annie Steel and Maud Diver to John Masters's *Nightrunners of Bengal* and J. G. Farrell's *The Siege of Krishnapur*, Amritsar is a far more common incident included in Indian fiction about the raj from Rao to Rushdie. An illustrative and powerful short story is Saadat Hasan Manto's concise "It happened in 1919" (in *Kingdom's End and Other Stories*). The significance of Kanpur to the British is explained by Charles Allen: "the memorial well at Kanpur, with its sculptured angel by Baron Marochetti, was British India's most sacred monument. 'Remember Kanpur,' scrawled on the walls of the *bibi khana* where over two hundred women and children were slaughtered in July 1857, remained a powerful rallying-cry among the British for years to come. Until shortly before World War II Indians were forbidden to enter the Memorial Gardens" (Charles Allen, *Raj* 11).

7 See Brantlinger's *Rule of Darkness* for a discussion of this.

8 The well as a symbol for the British is also stressed by Patrick Brantlinger's use of it as a chapter title in his book on colonial fiction, *Rule of Darkness*, and Michael Edwardes's use of it in one of the section headings in his book on the events of 1857 called *Red Year*.

9 The Parsee ritual, suggests Goonetilleke, is symbolic for Scott of the dead raj awaiting burial instructions from Whitehall (150).

10 This comes early in "The MacGregor House" section in the first AMS draft of *The Jewel in the Crown*: Austin: 1: unnumbered page.

11 This is reminiscent of one of Nehru's observations in a letter to Lord Linlithgow at the start of the war in 1939: "None of us, in India or England, dare remain in the old grooves or think in terms of past conditions. But events are moving so fast that sometimes I fear that they will overtake our slow-moving minds. There are all the elements of a Greek tragedy in the world situation today and we seem to be pushed along inevitably to a predestined end. You told me that I moved too much in the air. Probably you are right. But it is often possible to get a better view of the lie of the land from the heights than from the valleys" (quoted in Palling, 98).

12 Quoted in Moore, 174.

13 Rumours were rife that both the fat of pigs, which is unclean to Muslims, and the fat of cows, holy to Hindus, were the origin of the grease (e.g. see Said's Introduction to *Kim* 24).

14 *The Towers of Silence*: Austin: 6: 104.

15 There seems to be some confusion over Miss Sherwood's Christian name: Draper calls her Marcia, and Perkins names her Manuella. Scott took "Marcella" from Rupert Furneaux's 1963 account, *Massacre at Amritsar*.

16 These parallels are discussed by Weinbaum, 1992, 154.

17 For confirmation of Dyer's force of conviction and unrepentance, see Draper, 265.

18 Arterial sclerosis as a factor in Dyer's case is argued at D 156.

19 "Outside the Whale," in *Imaginary Homelands* 90.

[20] Rushdie, *Imaginary Homelands* 10. Rushdie speaks of a raj revival in the early eighties, and cites Scott's work as a part of it (87-101). Rushdie's view is probably true of television and cinema, but it is a strange distortion of recent literary history. Novels set in India, and linked with the raj, won the Booker prize in 1973, 1975, 1977, and 1981. To speak of a revival in the early eighties, when Rushdie himself won the literary award, therefore seems anachronistic. More particularly, to invoke Scott is absurd, except that his work—through no involvement of Scott's—had finally reached a mass audience after the success of the television adaptation of the *Quartet*. Scott himself had written consistently about the British in South East Asia from his first novel in 1952 to his last in 1977. For an extended response to Rushdie see Antony Copley's "The Politics of Illusion."

[21] Though this is certainly the case, sexual possibilities were frequent and diverse under the raj for those with the inclination and money or power to exploit them—as Perron finds out from the Red Shadow (for a detailed discussion see Hyam).

[22] Ruth Benedict usefully points out that "Racism did not get its currency in modern thought until it was applied to conflicts within Europe—first to class conflicts and then to national. . . . Racism was first formulated in conflicts between classes" (*Race and Racism* 111).

[23] Letter to Roland Gant, 9 May 1973, quoted in Moore, 172.

[24] Scott, proof of review of T. Zinkin's *Reporting India*, *TLS* 26 October 1962, Tulsa III: 6:75.

[25] Daphne, as the original "girl running" of the *Quartet* (and as Eve in Scott's image of lost paradise), is aptly seen as Pandora, the first woman according to Greek mythology.

[26] Scott's history begins with the Bibighar, just as many historians view recent Indo-British history beginning in 1857 with the cycle of Indian rebellion, British atrocities, Indian retaliation, and mutual recriminations. See Brantlinger 200-02 for a brief outline of this point.

CHAPTER FIVE

[1] This argument will be discussed in the next chapter as part of the reading of the image of "prisoners."

[2] And so, for example, Merrick's language is not only different from everyone else's but changes noticeably with each person he addresses: Sarah, Hari, Teddie, Ahmed, the prisoners, etc.

[3] The power of English lies in its ability to "unite" through its position as *the* language, but also to divide by its political position as the language of rulers, not subjects. Both aspects are alluded to in Mr. Das's ironic comment in Tom Stoppard's play *In the Native State*: "We have so many, many languages, you know, that English is the only language the nationalists can communicate in" (11-12). The use of English in India therefore provides Scott with a miniature case of his general concern with division and the failure to unify.

[4] Entry for "dialogism" in glossary by Emerson and Holquist, *DI* 426.

[5] *Man-bap* is also there in an exaggerated form in Ronnie's altercation with his mother in *A Passage to India*: "'Your sentiments are those of a god,' she said. . . . Trying to recover his temper he said, 'India likes gods.' 'And Englishmen like posing as gods.'" (62-63).

[6] Though it is also central to the civil service—see the chapter on the ICS in Charles Allen's *Plain Tales from the Raj*.

[1] E.g. an Indian novelist, Gita Mehta, debates the issue in her 1989 novel *Raj*, as does a European writer, Tom Stoppard, in his 1991 radio play, *In the Native State*; also, Manohar Malgonkar's 1972 novel *The Devil's Wind* (published while Scott was working on the *Quartet* and reviewed by him) uses as hero the scourge of English accounts of the revolt, Nana Sahib.

[2] Scott, Brown Spiral Notebook (Tulsa: II: 2: 3). Also quoted in R. Moore, 74.

[3] It will be shown later that he rejects the split by becoming "Philoctetes," the outcast—like one of the "outcasts" of the Hindu Sutras. Gorra (15-61), published after this chapter was written, gives a solid analysis of Hari's dual relation to England, ethnicity and Merrick's "situation."

[4] "India," corrected typescript, April 1969 (Tulsa: II: 9: 4: 2-4). In the *Quartet* this attitude to British parochialism is shown, for example, in Daphne's view of the "club mentality" (J 102).

[5] Scott may intend a parallel with the *Ramayana* in Hari's story: Hari is one of the names of Visnu, and Ram is an avatar of Visnu. In outline, the *Ramayana* is the story of "the son of a king . . . cheated out of his inheritance and forced into exile" (Smart, 160).

[6] Partly to illustrate the feeling of the smallness of their lives in the face of these forces, the characters are likened in the novels to small creatures: scorpions, butterflies, fireflies, snakes.

[7] Weinbaum, discussing the barriers between Indians and Anglo-Indians, writes: "the most significant imagery describing the division is that of Mayapore's black town and white cantonment, so carefully mapped out" (Weinbaum, 1981, 83). Towns were redesigned to enforce this separation after the 1857 rebellion (see Metcalf, 177-81).

[8] Mandir Gate is also the name of one of the gates of the Jallianwallah Bagh.

[9] Scott largely bases this on the common layout of Indian towns and cities under the British—for example Delhi is described by Palling thus: "Old Delhi, which sprang up nearly 1,000 years ago, is a maze of narrow lanes leading into courtyards crammed with traders and plastered with garish signs, whereas New Delhi, which was only completed in the 1930s, is centred on a grid of avenues and classical bungalows" (155). Benita Parry discusses these aspects of geometry and apartheid treasured by the British in India in a section entitled "Anglo-India in an Alien World," in her chapter on Flora Annie Steel in *Delusions and Discoveries* (121-30).

[10] In Granada's edition of *The Day of the Scorpion* (1973), it is "The Prisoner in the Fort."

[11] Perron tells little Bingham that "Edward" means "rich guard" (though it also connotes Edwardian and therefore is suggestive of the imperial past). Other names are also significant—for example, Scott is aware that both "Reginald" (Dyer) and "Ronald" (Merrick) mean "one with power who rules."

[12] This also applies to Indians like Kasim's elder son Sayed. And even Sarah senses "the presence of the next generation of her jailers" in the soldiers who visit Fenny (S 405).

[13] The myth occurs in the *Republic*, Book 7. Lyotard, explaining the myth of the cave in just the way that Scott uses it for the raj's mistaken view of itself and its glorified past, says that the allegory "recounts how and why men yearn for narratives and fail to recognize knowledge" (29).

[14] Sarah suggests the myth of the cave in her picture of the raj having "built a mansion without doors and windows, with no way in and no way out" (S 398).

[15] Repeated references also link Sarah's and Susan's gifts with the two blessings of the bungalow they live in ("grace" [see for example T 167] and "favour," respectively), much as Austen's Dashwood sisters personify sense and sensibility.

[16] These two creatures are also linked by what Sarah calls a "day of the snake," remembered by Mildred (S 69).

[17] In the imagery of the *Quartet* the scorpion gives way to the towers of silence in the third novel, where the raj, like the supine exposed bodies of the Parsees, will be left to the vultures.

[18] In the case of Barbie, Scott's choice of the butterfly image inevitably suggests Psyche and the Greek representation of the human soul as a butterfly. As such, members of the raj are portrayed as wanderers in search of love and union—as Psyche went in search of Cupid—but with little hope of success.

[19] Weinbaum traces the symbolic significance of both the ominous weather and the covering shawl—encapsulated in the rain cape present at Miss Crane's, Barbie's, and Daphne's tragedies (Weinbaum, 1992, 188). The significance of Barbie's song "Champagne Charlie" is that her father used to sing it (T 83) and had "Champagne tastes and beer income" (T 13), which is perhaps a comment on the over-weening pretensions of twentieth-century England, a small imperial country in decline at home and abroad.

[20] *The Towers of Silence*: Austin: 6: insert page "g6."

[21] This is succinctly expressed by Patterson (stating a coincidence of thought between Bakhtin, Lacan, and Heidegger): "The intrapersonal relation by which I become myself turns on the interpersonal relation to the other" (Patterson, 81).

[22] Edwina, desolate on the road from Dibrapur, stands as a similar "moral lesson" to a Gospel parable for Barbie, who imagines it as a tableau depicting Britain's attempts to heal divisions in India as having come "Too Late" (T 200). This "picture" of Edwina is Barbie's, and Scott's, substitute for "The Jewel in Her Crown."

[23] Scott is presumably commenting here on the English over-reliance in India on the intricate and powerful administration of the raj. He is alluding to Emerson's remark in "Self-reliance" that "An institution is the lengthened shadow of one man" (*Selected Writings* 138).

[24] The image of Parvati is thus superimposed by Barbie onto that of one of her pupils: "the nameless little girl; the unknown indian" (T 190).

[25] Apotheosis, or "god-making," was originally the ritual of raising a slain sacrificial saviour to heaven, to become a constellation among the stars—as Barbie pictures Teddie—or a part of God. Barbie's death is thus clearly seen, like Miss Crane's suttee, as a symbolic sacrifice (see Walker, 48).

[26] The importance of hands (particularly as symbols of union) is clear in the regularity with which they are mentioned—on one occasion for example hands are referred to eight times in the space of a page (T 66-67). To reflect this the cover of the Mayflower edition of *The Jewel in the Crown* is simply a picture of black and white hands touching.

[27] For Merrick this is a part of his self-made image: he becomes a war-hero through his attempt to save Teddie—however, it is worth remembering that we only hear the story of his bravery and self-sacrifice from Merrick himself.

[28] O'Flaherty, 262. Scott wrote that Parvati was the "female principle, called a shakti" of Siva on a sheet of typed notes taken from Isherwood's *Ramakrishna and His Disciples*.

The sheet is amongst the AMS notes he kept in his Brown Spiral Notebook (Tulsa: II: 2: 3).

[29] Ninian Smart writes: "It should be noted that these great Gods came to be thought of as alternative ways of expressing the truth about the supreme Being. It is not that there are two Gods: but rather, for the Hindu mind, worshippers may worship God either as Visnu or as Siva" (156).

[30] The link comes from Luke 10:19, "Behold I give unto you the power to tread on serpents and scorpions and over all the power of the enemy." This is complemented by Scott's use of the dancing Siva: "The right foot is the one that presses down on the crouching figure of the little demon" (J 384). Luke 11:11-12 is also pertinent here in joining images of the stone, the serpent and the scorpion.

[31] Review of Sasthi Brata, *My God Died Young: An Autobiography* (published by Hutchinson in 1968) (Tulsa: III: 1: 46); also quoted in Moore, 127.

[32] Ussher, Introduction to Sophocles, *Philoctetes*, 11.

[33] It might be objected here that Hari has nothing that the raj needs, whereas the Greeks needed the bow of Philoctetes. I would argue that Scott's point is that an understanding of Hari's experience *is* needed to alleviate future tension and hostility. The rejection of Indo-Anglians is a factor in the racism of the sixties and seventies.

CHAPTER SEVEN

[1] *The Towers of Silence*: Austin: 6: insert page "nnn." The passage comes near the start of Book two, after the announcements in *The Times*. The closest discussion of this "malign influence" in the published novel comes near the start of "The Silver in the Mess," when Barbie remembers her childhood games being watched over by a figure who anticipates the sinister presence of Merrick: "the icy little hand would touch her low down on the back of her neck, the hand of the invisible guest, the demon-spirit of the party who knew the answers to all the conundrums and puzzles and who presided over the gathering with a thrilling kind of malice, totting up the scores and marking down for ridicule, if not worse, special victims . . ." (T 167).

Barbie often senses this spirit throughout *The Towers of Silence*, from "a curious emanation, of a sickness" (T 17) up to when she meets Merrick and gasps "both at the sight of a man and at the noxious emanation" (T 369). This is opposed to the "goodness in the air," the *prana* ("vital breath," Stutley, 172) that Barbie associates with roses—and therefore with Sarah, Mabel, and Gaffur (T 332).

[2] See the essays in Bhabha's *The Location of Culture*.

[3] There are echoes of Hari in Merrick's attraction to Aziz. Scott even creates similarities of circumstance: for example, when Aziz returns from Merrick's room, Khansamar "noticed that there were marks on [Aziz's] face and that he had been bathing them" (D 566).

[4] See glossary in O'Flaherty.

[5] Conrad speaks of the idea at the back of civilization (*Heart of Darkness*, 10) redeeming its "conquest of the earth." The idea is that of the introduction of education, efficiency, civilization, and "enlightenment"—everything Kurtz's original report proposed, which is a product of the West's belief in its humanity. This belief grew alongside humanism's denial of God in the nineteenth century. In parallel with, and also almost in anticipation of, Darwin's theory of evolution, many writers, and in particular Auguste Comte in his *Positivist Philosophy* of 1830, argued that societies developed and progressed to

different stages, from an animalistic egoism to a moral altruism. From this, arises the West's self-image as moral guardian, torch-bearer, and pedagogue.

[6] Scott is not against committing oneself to a viewpoint. As a novelist he felt that one had to have a "firm opinion" and express it (see M 57); but he wrote against commitment that spilt over into dogmatism or unswerving self-belief that eschewed uncertainty and compromise as weaknesses.

[7] Sartre, *Being and Nothingness*, 481-553.

[8] In pursuing these ideas, we are not concerned with establishing the reasons for Sartre's views, an explanation of which is beyond our scope, but with their similarity to Merrick's views and the actions that follow from them—actions which reveal, for Scott, a misuse of freedom and an incorrect negation of love. Also, Sartre's views changed considerably, as can be noted from the contrast between the accepting attitude to humanism expressed in his 1946 essay (and its title) "L'Existentialisme est un humanisme" and his later denigratory remark, "Humanism is the counterpart of racism" (quoted in Young, 123). The discussion in this chapter is primarily concerned with views expressed in *Being and Nothingness*.

[9] Scott himself despaired of "the obstinate refusal of people of one colour to recognize their own aspirations in people of another. Meanwhile, presumably, we must all limp on; wearing the thick boot of envy at the end of one leg and the iron of contempt on the other" (review of *Rampal and His Family* by Ursula Sharma, for the *TLS*, quoted Moore, 138). Spurling uses the final image for a chapter title in her biography of Scott.

[10] See the essays by Weinbaum (1978, 111, endnote 11) and Boyer (65).

[11] Here is an allusion to the start of *The Prelude* and its allusion to the end of *Paradise Lost*. Scott suggests for Merrick both the vision of a new world spread before Adam and Eve, and the certainty of Wordsworth's self-belief: "The earth is all before me. With a heart / Joyous, nor scared at its own liberty, / I look about; and should the guide I choose / Be nothing better than a wandering cloud / I cannot miss my way" (*The Prelude* 1805, 1: 15-19).

[12] Merrick tries to surmount the social ambit of his background and to build an identity on stereotypes of the dependable British colonial ruler. He remains, however, a split subject whose alter-ego at times appears, Hyde-like, under cover of the night and disguised in Pathan robes.

[13] Holquist on Bakhtin, in Hernadi ed. 207.

[14] In Merrick's case, it can be added that he distorts this by consciously drawing his own lines and attaching judgments of superiority and inferiority to the two sides.

[15] Scott made this point more strongly in an earlier draft of *The Towers of Silence*. For example, Merrick says: "I hadn't appreciated what the difference was between me and the boys in the adventure stories" (*The Towers of Silence*: Austin: 6: 659).

[16] Again, while this is a paradox on the surface, it is not uncommon, and Merrick's attempt to present himself as an ideal of a superior social group is not unusual, as noted by Erving Goffman: "One of the richest sources of data on the presentation of idealized performances is the literature on social mobility. In . . . most stratified societies there is an idealization of the higher strata and some aspiration on the part of those in low places to move to higher ones. (One must be careful to appreciate that this involves not merely a desire for a prestigeful place but also a desire for a place close to the sacred centre of the shared values of the society.) Commonly we find that upward mobility involves the presentation of proper performances . . ." (45).

157

[17] Scott in conversation with Weinbaum, quoted in Rao 118.

[18] In the case of dharma this is clear from our previous notes about the word, but less so with karma: "Some sociologists believe that belief in the doctrine of Karma and Rebirth is basic for the functioning of the caste system. This is because such a belief is supposed to reconcile a man to the low status ascribed to him by caste" (Paranjpe 51).

[19] Allen 1977, 45.

[20] The image of the White Man appears both in Kipling's fiction, such as *Kim*, and in poems such as "The Road that the White Men Tread."

CONCLUSION

[1] Goonetilleke, 15; Bergonzi, 225; Anthony Burgess, 116; Storm Jameson in correspondence to Scott (Tulsa: I: 9: 24).

[2] Ghose, review of *The Day of the Scorpion* in *Western Mail,* 7 September 1968; Narayan is quoted in Moore, 126.

WORKS CITED

(The place of publication is London unless otherwise stated.)

Achebe, Chinua. "An Image of Africa: Racism in Conrad's *Heart of Darkness.*" *Hopes and Impediments: Selected Essays 1965-1987.* Heinemann, 1988. 1-13.

Ali, Tariq. "Fiction as History, History as Fiction." *Illustrated Weekly of India* 8 July 1984.

Allen, Charles. *Raj: A Scrapbook of British India, 1877-1947.* Andre Deutsch, 1977.

———, ed. *Plain Tales from the Raj.* BBC Books, 1992.

Althusser, Louis. "Ideology and Ideological State Apparatuses." *Essays on Ideology.* Verso, 1971.

Anderson, Benedict. *Imagined Communities: Reflections on the Origin and Spread of Nationalism.* Rev. ed. Verso, 1991.

Aristotle. *Poetics.* Trans. K. A. Telford. Chicago: Gateway, 1961.

Ashcroft, Bill, Gareth Griffiths, and Helen Tiffin. *The Empire Writes Back.* Routledge, 1989.

Bakhtin, Mikhail M. *The Dialogic Imagination.* Ed. Michael Holquist. Trans. Caryl Emerson and Michael Holquist. Austin: University of Texas Press, 1981.

———. *Speech Genres and Other Late Essays.* Ed. Caryl Emerson and Michael Holquist. Trans. Vern W. McGee. Austin: University of Texas Press, 1986.

———. *Art and Answerability.* Ed. Michael Holquist and Vadim Liapunov. Trans. Vadim Liapunov. Supplement trans. Kenneth Brostrom. Austin: University of Texas Press, 1990.

———. *Problems of Dostoevsky's Poetics.* Trans. and ed. Caryl Emerson. Manchester: Manchester University Press, 1984.

———. *Rabelais and his World.* Trans. Hélène Iswolsky. Bloomington: Indiana University Press, 1984.

Ballhatchet, Kenneth. *Race, Sex, and Class under the Raj.* Weidenfeld and Nicholson, 1980.

Bannerjee, Jacqueline. "A Living Legacy: An Indian View of Paul Scott's India." *London Magazine.* April-May 1980: 97-104.

Batchelor, John. *The Edwardian Novelists.* Duckworth, 1982.

Benedict, Ruth. *Race and Racism.* 1942. Rpt. with introduction by John Rex. Routledge & Kegan Paul, 1983.

Bennett, Tony. *Formalism and Marxism*. Methuen, 1979.

Bergonzi, Bernard. *The Situation of the Novel*. 2nd ed. Macmillan, 1979.

Bhabha, Homi. *The Location of Culture*. Routledge, 1994.

Boyer, Allen. "Love, Sex, and History in *The Raj Quartet*." *Modern Language Quarterly* 46 (1985): 64-80.

Bradbury, Malcolm. *The Social Context of Modern English Literature*. Oxford: Blackwell, 1971.

———, ed. *The Novel Today*. Fontana, 1977.

———, and James McFarlane, eds. *Modernism*. Harmondsworth: Pelican, 1976.

Brantlinger, Patrick. *Rule of Darkness: British Literature and Imperialism, 1830-1914*. Ithaca: Cornell University Press, 1988.

Burgess, Anthony. *Ninety-Nine Novels*. Allison and Busby, 1984.

Butterfield, Herbert. *The Whig Interpretation of History*. 1935. Rpt. Bell and Son, 1963.

Carthill, A. L. *The Legacy of Liberalism*. Allan and Co., 1924.

Chaudhuri, Nirad C. *The Autobiography of an Unknown Indian*. 1951. Bombay: Jaico Publishing House, 1976.

Chronicle of the Twentieth Century. Essex: Longman, 1988.

Clark, Katerina and Michael Holquist. *Mikhail Bakhtin*. Cambridge, MA: Harvard University Press, 1987.

Colwell, Danny. "'I am your Mother and your Father': Paul Scott's *Raj Quartet* and the Dissolution of Imperial Identity.'" *Writing India 1757-1990*. Ed. Bart Moore-Gilbert. Manchester: Manchester University Press, 1996. 213-35.

Connolly, Cyril. *Enemies of Promise*. 1938. Rev. ed. 1948. Harmondsworth: Penguin, 1961.

Conrad, Joseph. *Heart of Darkness*. 1902. Harmondsworth: Penguin, 1973.

Copley, Antony. "The Politics of Illusion: Paul Scott's *The Raj Quartet*." *Indo-British Review* 11 (1984): 58-73.

Couto, Maria. "Clinging to the Wreckage: Raj Fictions." *Encounter* Sept-Oct. 1984: 34-40.

Cox, C. B. *The Free Spirit*. Oxford: Oxford University Press, 1963.

Crews, Frederick C. "A Passage to India." Rutherford, 78-89.

Cronin, Richard. *Imagining India*. Macmillan, 1989.

Draper, Alfred. *Amritsar: The Massacre that Ended the Raj*. Cassell, Macmillan, 1981.

Dummett, Michael, and Ann Dummett. "The Role of Government in Britain's Racial Crisis." Husband, 132-67.

Eagleton, Terry. *Literary Theory: An Introduction*. Oxford: Blackwell, 1983.

Edwardes, Michael. *Red Year: The Indian Rebellion of 1857*. Cardinal, Sphere, 1975.

Emerson, Ralph Waldo. *Selected Writings of Emerson*. Ed. Donald McQuade. New York: Random House, 1981.

Fanon, Frantz. *The Wretched of the Earth*. Trans. Constance Farrington. Intro. Jean-Paul Sartre. Harmondsworth: Penguin, 1967.

Forster, E. M. *A Passage to India*. 1924. Harmondsworth: Penguin, 1985.

———. *The Hill of Devi*. 1953. Harmondsworth: Penguin, 1965.

Foucault, Michel. *The Foucault Reader*. Ed. Paul Rabinow. Harmondsworth: Penguin, 1991.

Gates, Henry Louis, Jr., ed. *"Race," Writing and Difference*. Chicago: University of Chicago Press, 1986.

Goffman, Erving. *The Presentation of Self in Everyday Life*. 1959. Harmondsworth: Pelican, 1971.

Gooneratne, Yasmin. "The Expatriate Experience: The Novels of Ruth Prawer Jhabvala and Paul Scott." *The British and Irish Novel since 1960*. Ed. James Acheson. Macmillan, 1991. 47-65.

Goonetilleke, D. C. R. A. *Images of the Raj: South Asia in the Literature of Empire*. Macmillan, 1988.

Gorra, Michael. *After Empire: Scott, Naipaul, Rushdie*. Chicago: University of Chicago Press, 1997.

Green, Martin. *Dreams of Adventure, Deeds of Empire*. New York: Basic Books, 1979.

Gregory, Richard L. *The Oxford Companion to the Mind*. Oxford: Oxford UP, 1987.

Hawthorn, Jeremy. *A Concise Glossary of Contemporary Literary Theory*. Edward Arnold, 1992.

Hobson, J. A. *Imperialism: A Study*. 1902. George Allen and Unwin, 1948.

Hodson, H. V. *Twentieth-Century Empire*. Faber, 1948.

Holquist, Michael. *Dialogism*. Routledge, 1990.

———. "The Inevitability of Stereotype: Colonialism in *The Great Gatsby*." *The Rhetoric of Interpretation and the Interpretation of Rhetoric*. Ed. Paul Hernadi. Durham: Duke University Press, 1989. 201-20.

Husband, Charles, ed. *"Race" in Britain: Continuity and Change*. 2nd ed. Hutchinson University Press, 1972.

Huttenback, R. A. "The British Empire as a 'White Man's Country': Racial Attitudes and Immigration Legislation in the Colonies of White Settlers." *Journal of British Studies* 13.1 (1973): 108-37.

Hyam, Ronald. *Empire and Sexuality: The British Experience*. Manchester: Manchester University Press, 1990.

Kipling, Rudyard. *Kim*. 1901. Harmondsworth: Penguin, 1987.

Konvitz, M. E., and S. E. Whicher. *The Definitive Edition of Rudyard Kipling's Verse.* Hodder and Stoughton, 1944.

———. *Emerson: A Collection of Critical Essays.* Englewood Cliffs, NJ: Prentice-Hall, 1962.

The Koran. Trans. N. J. Dawood. Rev. ed. Harmondsworth: Penguin, 1974.

Lyotard, Jean-Francois. *The Postmodern Condition: A Report on Knowledge.* Trans. Geoff Bennington and Brian Massumi. Manchester: Manchester University Press, 1984.

Mahood, M. M. "Paul Scott's Guardians." *The Yearbook of English Studies* 13 (1983): 244-58.

Manto, Saadat Hasan. *Kingdom's End and Other Stories.* Trans. Khalid Hasan. Harmondsworth: Penguin, 1987.

McHale, Brian. *Postmodernist Fiction.* Methuen, 1987.   .

Mehta, Gita. *Karma Cola: Marketing the Mystic East.* New York: Simon, 1981.

———. *Raj.* New York: Random House, 1989.

Messent, Peter. *New Readings of the American Novel.* Macmillan, 1990.

Metcalf, Thomas. *Ideologies of the Raj.* Cambridge: Cambridge University Press, 1994.

Mills, Sara, et al. *Feminists Reading: Feminist Readings.* Brighton: Harvester, 1989.

Moore, Robin. *Paul Scott's Raj.* Heinemann, 1990.

Natanson, Maurice. *A Critique of Jean-Paul Sartre's Ontology.* New York: Haskell House, 1972.

O'Flaherty, Wendy, trans. *Hindu Myths.* Harmondsworth: Penguin, 1975.

Orwell, George. *Burmese Days.* 1935. *The Penguin Complete Novels of George Orwell.* Harmondsworth: Penguin, 1983.

———. *Coming Up for Air.* 1938. *The Penguin Complete Novels of George Orwell.* Harmondsworth: Penguin, 1983.

Osborne, John. *Look Back in Anger.* Faber, 1960.

Palling, Bruce. *A Literary Companion: India.* John Murray, 1992.

Paranjpe, A. C. *Caste, Prejudice and the Individual.* Lalvani, Bombay, 1970.

Parry, Benita. *Delusions and Discoveries: Studies of India in the British Imagination 1880-1930.* Harmondsworth: Allen Lane, 1972.

Patterson, David. *Literature and Spirit: Essays on Bakhtin and His Contemporaries.* Lexington: University Press of Kentucky, 1988.

Perkins, Roger. *The Amritsar Legacy: Golden Temple to Caxton Hall, the Story of a Killing.* Chippenham: Picton, 1989.

Plato. *The Republic.* Trans A. D. Lindsay. Dent and Sons, 1976.

Powell, J. Enoch. "Myth and Reality." *Freedom and Reality.* Ed. John Wood. Batsford, 1969. 238-57.

Rao, K. B. *Paul Scott.* Boston: Twayne, 1980.

Rubin, David. *After the Raj: British Novels of India since 1947.* Hanover, NH: University Press of New England, 1986.

Rushdie, Salman. *Imaginary Homelands: Essays and Criticism 1981-1991.* Harmondsworth: Granta, 1992.

Rutherford, Andrew, ed. *Twentieth Century Interpretations of "A Passage to India."* Englewood Cliffs, NJ: Prentice-Hall, 1970.

Said, Edward. *Orientalism.* 1978. Harmondsworth: Penguin, 1991.

———. *The World, the Text and the Critic.* 1984. Verso, 1991.

———. Introduction to *Kim.* By Rudyard Kipling. Harmondsworth: Penguin, 1987.

———. *Culture and Imperialism.* Chatto and Windus, 1993.

Sartre, Jean-Paul. *Being and Nothingness.* Trans. Hazel E. Barnes. New York: Philosophical Library, 1956.

Scheick, William J. *The Slender Human Word: Emerson's Artistry in Prose.* Knoxville: University of Tennessee Press, 1978.

Scholes, Robert. Foreword. *The Fantastic.* By Tzvetan Todorov. Trans. Richard Howard. Ithaca: Cornell University Press, 1973. v-xi.

Scanlan, Margaret. *Traces of Another Time: History and Politics in Postwar British Fiction.* Princeton: Princeton University Press, 1990.

Schwarz, Bill. "An Englishman Abroad . . . And At Home: The Case of Paul Scott." *New Formations* 17 (Summer 1992): 95-106.

Scott, Paul. *My Appointment with the Muse.* Ed. Shelley C. Reece. Heinemann, 1986.

———. *Johnny Sahib.* Viking, 1952.

———. *The Alien Sky.* 1953. Grafton, 1974.

———. *A Male Child.* 1956. Grafton, 1974.

———. *The Mark of the Warrior.* 1958. Panther, 1979.

———. *The Chinese Love Pavillion.* 1960. Granada, 1973.

———. *The Birds of Paradise.* 1962. Grafton, 1969.

———. *The Bender.* 1963. Panther, 1975.

———. *The Corrida at San Felíu.* 1964. Pan, 1989.

———. *The Raj Quartet: The Jewel in the Crown, The Day of the Scorpion, The Towers of Silence, A Division of the Spoils.* Heinemann, 1976.

———. *Staying On.* Grafton, 1978.

Sharpe, Jenny. *Allegories of Empire: the Figure of Woman in the Colonial Text.* Minneapolis: Minnesota University Press, 1993.

Silver, Brenda R. "Periphrasis, Power and Rape in *A Passage to India.*" *Novel* 21 (1988): 86-105.

Smart, Ninian. *The Religious Experience of Mankind.* Collins, 1977.

Solomon, Robert C. *From Rationalism to Existentialism.* 1972. Washington: University Press of America, 1985.

Sophocles. *Philoctetes.* Trans. R. G. Ussher. Wiltshire: Aris and Phillips, 1990.

Spurling, Hilary. *Paul Scott: A Life.* Hutchinson, 1990.

Stoppard, Tom. *In the Native State.* Faber, 1991.

Stutley, Margaret. *Hinduism: The Eternal Law.* Wellingborough, Northamptonshire: Aquarian Press, 1985.

Suleri, Sara. "The Geography of *A Passage to India.*" *Literature in the Modern World.* Ed. Dennis Walder. Oxford: Oxford University Press, 1990.

Swinden, Patrick. *Paul Scott: Images of India.* Macmillan, 1980.

Thompson, Edward. *An Indian Day.* 1927. Macmillan, 1933.

Todorov, Tzvetan. *Mikhail Bakhtin: The Dialogical Principle.* Trans. Wlad Godzich. Minneapolis: University of Minnesota Press, 1984.

Trevelyan, Raleigh. *The Golden Oriole: Childhood, Family and Friends in India.* Oxford: Oxford University Press, 1988.

Vico, Giovanni Battista. *New Science.* Trans T. Bergin and M. Fisch. 2nd ed. Ithaca: Cornell University Press, 1948.

Walker, Barbara G. *The Woman's Encyclopedia of Myths and Secrets.* San Francisco: Harper and Row, 1983.

Walsh, William. *Indian Literature in English.* Essex: Longman, 1990.

Watson, J. R. *English Poetry of the Romantic Period 1789-1830.* 2nd ed. Essex: Longman, 1992.

Weinbaum, Francine S. "Paul Scott's India: *The Raj Quartet.*" *Critique* 20 (1978): 100-110.

———. "Psychological Defences and Thwarted Union in *The Raj Quartet.*" *Literature and Psychology* 31 (1981): 75-87.

———. *Paul Scott: A Critical Study.* Austin: University of Texas Press, 1992.

White, Allon. "Bakhtin, Sociolinguistics, and Deconstruction." *The Theory of Reading.* Ed. Frank Gloversmith. Brighton: Harvester Press, 1984. 123-46

White, Hayden. *Metahistory: The Historical Imagination in Nineteenth-Century Europe.* Baltimore: Johns Hopkins University Press, 1973.

Wolpert, Stanley. *A New History of India.* 4th ed. Oxford: Oxford University Press, 1993.

Woolf, Virginia. *A Room of One's Own.* 1929. Grafton, 1977.

———. *Orlando.* 1928. Hogarth, 1978.

———. "Modern Fiction." 1919. *Twentieth-Century Literary Criticism.* Ed. David Lodge. Essex: Longman, 1972 86-91.

Wordsworth, William. 1805. *The Prelude.* Ed. Ernest De Selincourt and Stephen Gill. Oxford: Oxford University Press, 1970.

Yalland, Z. *Traders and Nabobs: The British in Cawnpore 1765-1857.* Salisbury: Michael Russell, 1987.

Young, Robert. *White Mythologies: Writing History and the West.* Routledge, 1990.

ENGLISH LITERARY STUDIES MONOGRAPH SERIES

ENGLISH LITERARY STUDIES publishes peer-reviewed monographs (usual length, 45,000-60,000 words) on the literatures written in English. The Series is open to a wide range of scholarly and critical methodologies, and it considers for publication bibliographies, scholarly editions, and historical and critical studies of significant authors, texts, and issues. ELS publishes two to five monographs annually.